To inspire ambition, to stimulate the imagination, to provide the inquiring mind with accurate information told in an interesting style, and thus lead into broader fields of knowledge—such is the purpose of this work

The New
BOOK OF KNOWLEDGE
Volume Two

Made and Printed in Great Britain by The Amalgamated Press, Ltd.

EXQUISITE GEMS of the INSECT WORLD

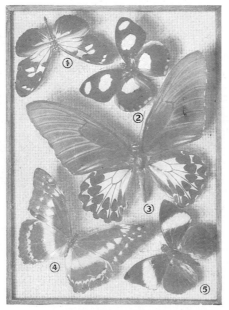

KEY TO PRECEDING COLOUR PLATE

OF all insects the butterflies wear the most brilliant costumes, especially those dressed for tropical climates. The photograph in the preceding page was made in natural colours from actual specimens gathered in distant lands. Each is identified through the numbered key-picture here at the left.

In the high forests of Peru was caught *Heliconius burneyi* (1), which, like most other tropical butterflies, has no popular English name. His orange-spotted neighbour, *Catonephela numilia* (2), came from the Amazon valley. A Dutch collector in the island of Sumatra, East Indies, captured the great " bird-winged " butterfly (3) called *Ornithoptera vandepolli*. The blue beauty of *Morpho cypris* (4) is characteristic of a famous tribe some members of which have a wing-spread of eight inches or more. This one began life in the lofty woodlands of the Republic of Colombia. When *Agria claudiens* (5) arrived in this country he was labelled from Para, Brazil.

Why have butterflies developed such brilliant colours ? There are many answers and much that still puzzles scientists. Butterflies of the heliconid type (1) contain bitter liquids distasteful to birds, who quickly learn to recognize the warning colours and to leave them alone. Some butterflies, like numbers 2 and 4, exhibit their bright colours only in flight when they may serve to attract a mate. At rest on a twig with wings folded up over their backs, showing only the dull brown undersides, these butterflies are extremely difficult to distinguish from their surroundings.

EXQUISITE GEMS OF THE INSECT WORLD

See text overleaf.

THE NEW BOOK OF KNOWLEDGE

A Pictorial Treasury of Reading
& Reference for Young and Old

Edited by

SIR JOHN HAMMERTON

Editor, Universal Encyclopedia, Universal History of the World, Peoples of All Nations
Countries of the World, Encyclopedia of Modern Knowledge, New Popular Educator

With Eight Thousand Illustrations including
nearly Eight Hundred in Colour & Photogravure

*Complete in Ten Volumes including Easy Reference Fact-Index
Study Outlines and Topics Guide to Every Day of the Year*

VOLUME TWO: BIB—CHIC

THE WAVERLEY BOOK COMPANY LTD.
Farringdon Street, London, E.C.4

HERE AND THERE IN THIS VOLUME

*At odd times when you are just looking for " something interesting to read," with-
out any special plan in mind, this list will help you. With this as a guide, you
may wander through storyland, visit far-away countries, meet famous people of
ancient and modern times, review history's most memorable incidents, explore the
marvels of Nature and science, play games—in short, find whatever suits your fancy at
the moment. This list is not intended to serve as a table of contents, an index, or a
study-guide. For these turn to the Fact-Index and Study Outlines in Volume Ten.*

TALES FOR THE STORY HOUR

	PAGE
MAKING FRIENDS WITH THE BIRDS	529
THE STORY OF THE PILGRIM'S PROGRESS	720
WHAT SINBAD FOUND OUT IN THE DESERT ..	781
THE STORY OF ALICE'S AMAZING ADVENTURES ..	845
HOW BIG-HEAD SLEW THE CAVE-BEAR ..	886
THE STORY OF DON QUIXOTE'S ADVENTURES ..	903
THE KNIGHT'S TALE OF PALAMON AND ARCITE ..	931
THE CLERK'S TALE OF PATIENT GRISELDA ..	932

HIGH-LIGHTS IN HISTORY'S PAGEANT

THE STORY OF THE BOER WAR	564
THE LAND OF THE CELTS AND GAELS	655
GREATER BRITAIN BEYOND THE SEAS	662
EUROPE'S BULWARK AGAINST ASIA	743
CABOT'S TRAVELS TO THE NEW WORLD	754
STIRRING STORY OF CANADA'S PAST	803
THE STORY OF ROME'S GREATEST RIVAL	847
WHERE THE BOLD BARON LIVED IN STATE ..	855

SOME FAMOUS MEN AND WOMEN

BISMARCK, THE IRON CHANCELLOR	535
BLAKE, THE GREAT ADMIRAL	544
BLÉRIOT, CONQUEROR OF THE CHANNEL ..	547
BLONDIN, INTREPID TIGHT-ROPE WALKER ..	550
ANNE BOLEYN, TRAGIC QUEEN	566
GENERAL BOOTH OF THE SALVATION ARMY ..	590
GEORGE BORROW, FRIEND OF GIPSIES	601
JAMES BOSWELL, DR. JOHNSON'S BIOGRAPHER ..	605
ENGLAND'S FIRST GREAT CHEMIST	613
BRADMAN OF TEST MATCH FAME	621
TYCHO BRAHE, PIONEER ASTRONOMER ..	622
ARISTIDE BRIAND, STATESMAN OF FRANCE ..	641
ROBERT BRUCE, HERO OF A LEGEND	685
BRUNEL, CREATOR OF HISTORIC SHIPS ..	689
JOHN BUCHAN, AUTHOR AND ADMINISTRATOR ..	693
THE FOUNDER OF THE ROMAN EMPIRE ..	759
CARLYLE—SAGE, PROPHET, AND PREACHER ..	833
CARNEGIE, MAGNATE AND PHILANTHROPIST ..	835

THE WORLD AT WORK

THE BIOGRAPHY OF A LOAF OF BREAD	633
THE BRIDGE-BUILDER AND HIS WORK	645
BUILDING GIANTS WITH BONES OF STEEL ..	703
MAN-MADE RIVERS ACROSS THE LAND	809
THE LOVELINESS WE TREAD UPON	839

THE WORLD AT PLAY

HOW BILLIARDS IS PLAYED	495
FROM LOG RAFT TO RACING YACHT	557
BOWLS : HISTORIC LAWN GAME	610
BOXING : A MANLY ART	611
GOOD CITIZENS IN THE MAKING	615
THE LORE AND LURE OF CAMPING	788
CHESS : ANCIENT GAME OF PURE SKILL ..	950

IN THE PLANT AND ANIMAL WORLD

	PAGE
MARVELS OF THE SCIENCE OF LIFE	500
OUR CHARMING FRIENDS IN FEATHERS	508
VANQUISHED MONARCHS OF THE PLAINS	536
LOOKING INTO THE HEART OF A GROWING PLANT ..	606
ELVES AND SPRITES OF INSECT LIFE	734
THE STORY OF THE CABBAGE	747
CACTUS : PLANT OF THE ARID REGIONS	756
THE SHAGGY SHIP OF THE DESERT	778
PUSS IN PICTURE AND IN STORY	862
MOST USEFUL OF DOMESTIC ANIMALS	877

SIGN-POSTS TO LITERATURE AND ARTS

THE GREATEST BOOK IN THE WORLD	489
THE BRONTËS AND THEIR STORY	680
ROBERT BROWNING : VICTORIAN POET	684
THE INSPIRED TINKER OF ELSTOW	719
SCOTLAND'S PLOUGHMAN POET	730
CREATOR OF " ALICE IN WONDERLAND " ..	843
CATHEDRALS IN THE MODERN SCENE	867
THE MAN WHO WROTE " DON QUIXOTE " ..	902
THE FATHER OF ENGLISH POETRY	927
CHESTERTON : MASTER OF PARADOX	954

MARVELS OF SCIENCE AND INVENTION

THE BLOODSTREAM IN OUR BODIES	551
THE WONDER OF A PRINTED BOOK	580
FROM ANCIENT SANDAL TO MODERN SHOE ..	593
MARVELLOUS MACHINERY OF THE BRAIN ..	623
SENDING MESSAGES UNDER THE SEA	749
MACHINES THAT DO DIFFICULT SUMS	767
CAMOUFLAGE : THE ART OF CONCEALMENT ..	786
CELLULOSE : WONDROUS SUBSTANCE OF THE MODERN WORLD	892
THE SCIENCE OF MODERN MIRACLES	937

GLIMPSES OF LANDS ACROSS THE SEAS

ANDEAN LAND OF SUN AND SNOW	567
SOUTH AMERICA'S LARGEST COUNTRY	628
THE " SUNSET GATEWAY " OF CANADA	659
BULGARIA, LAND OF PEASANTS	715
A COUNTRY IN A JUNGLE-CLAD VALLEY	727
DOMINION OF PINE AND PRAIRIE	794

RAMBLES THROUGH FACT-LAND

EDUCATION OF THE BLIND	548
HOW TO KEEP A SET OF BOOKS	578
STEPS IN THE MAKING OF A MODERN BOOK ..	584
MUD PIES WE USE IN BUILDING	643
A WORD-PICTURE OF OUR HOMELAND	675
STORE-HOUSE OF THE WORLD'S TREASURES ..	677
CAVES : NATURE'S HIDDEN ARCHITECTURE ..	882

CAN YOU ANSWER THESE QUESTIONS?

Since unnumbered thousands of questions are answered in each one of our ten volumes, this page is intended merely as a sample of the pleasure and instruction that may be obtained by discovering interesting facts in this volume and passing them on to others in question form. There are many thousands more for you to draw upon as tests in General Knowledge.

	PAGE
When were table forks invented ?	856
Why do birds migrate ?	509
What is the difference between stalagmites and stalactites ?	882
What mighty emperor played with toys ?	916
How often is a census taken in Britain ?	896
What was the " elixir of life " ?	944
Is there any difference between a bison and a buffalo ?	536
Do living creatures ever come from dead matter ?	504
What were the centaurs ?	897
What is a caisson ?	764
How is cement made ?	894
How long does a hen's egg take to hatch ?	518
Who was the " ploughman poet " ?	730
Who are the " three B's of music " ?	622
Which is the world's highest capital ?	567
What empire includes a quarter of the globe ?	663
Where is the largest unexplored area in the Western Hemisphere ?	628
What does the word " biscuit " mean ?	535
What is the science of Genetics ?	504
Why did the ancient Egyptians put straw in their bricks ?	643
What is the Apocrypha ?	491
What is the Periodic Table ?	940
What town was called the " Protestant Rome " ?	773
How are book sizes indicated ?	583
Who thought windmills were giants ?	903
Why do Buddhists never take life of any sort ?	699
What animals eat their own weight of food in a day ?	510
How did Bombay become British ?	572
What king's heart went to battle without him ?	686
When was the Bible first translated into English ?	492
How much of your body is blood ?	551
How many chemical elements are there ?	937
Of what English king was it said: "he never said a foolish thing nor did a wise one " ?	919
How many legs has a caterpillar ?	865
Why should a person who has fainted be laid flat ?	553
Why was the strait called the Bosporus given that name ?	603
How do the tulip and crocus get a start over other plants in spring ?	714
Which country produces most of the world's supply of borax ?	596

	PAGE
How did the Black Death help to end the Middle Ages ?	541
What is meant by hybridization ?	725
How can you read with your fingers ?	549
What famous Scottish king was inspired by the example of a spider ?	685
What animal has headlights ?	503
Why are butterflies given the scientific name of lepidoptera ?	734
How many species of birds are there ?	520
What is the difference between a mixture and a chemical compound ?	937
Do birds resemble reptiles ?	508
How many colours or pigments are present in a bird's feathers ?	519
What part of the brain controls speech ?	626
What is a building society ?	713
Did birds ever have teeth or fingers ?	509
Who was Buffalo Bill ?	702
What is a cantilever bridge ?	647
Why is there a figure of Britannia on the backs of our pennies ?	658
What makes bread " rise " ?	633
Where do we get the hairs used in brushes?	682
How is the pressure of the atmosphere used to stop a train ?	627
How many people are there in the British Empire ?	662
What is " camouflage " ?	786
What is the origin of the hot cross bun ?	718
Why do shops have cash registers ?	851
Why are steel rods often embedded in concrete ?	710
Who was the "Old Man of Cro-Magnon"?	884
What is " shammy " leather ?	911
When was the Bronze Age ?	681
What does the term " stalemate " mean ?	952
Which is the highest mountain in the British Isles ?	676
What is the origin of the word " bunkum " ?	718
How did Brindley halve the price of coal in Manchester ?	653
Was Britain ever part of the Continent ?	675
In what languages was the Bible written ?	491
How does the sail make the boat go along?	560
What is the difference between a biography and an autobiography ?	499
Who puts butter in his tea ?	733
Do all birds sing ?	513
What is the " Devil's Bible " ?	494
Who first crossed the English Channel in an aeroplane ?	547
Who was the Mad Hatter ?	845

COLOUR and GRAVURE PLATES and PAGES
IN THIS VOLUME

Exquisite Gems of the Insect World .. Frontispiece

Birds : Some Fine Specimens of British Birds' Eggs .. .. facing p. 512

Birds : Beauty in the World of Wings .. pp. 521–528

Borneo : Barbaric Finery of the Young Dyaks .. .. facing p. 600

Borneo : Chieftain of Borneo Armed for the Battle .. .. „ „ 601

Boy Scouts : Badges of Distinction Awarded to Boy Scouts .. .. „ „ 620

Bridge : How the Bridge-builder Conquers Space .. .. „ „ 645

British Empire : Deeds that Won Britain's Empire.. .. .. pp. 665–672

British Isles : Map showing heights and depths, railways, canals, etc. .. facing p. 676

Building : London's New Giants Built of Stone and Steel .. .. .. pp. 705–708

Butterfly : The Life-History of a Butterfly facing p. 732

Butterflies of the British Isles .. .. „ „ 736

Further British Butterflies, and Moths from all Parts of the World .. .. „ „ 737

Cairo : Midday Sunshine in a Cairo Side Street .. .. „ „ 764

Cairo : Looking across the Roofs and Minarets of Cairo .. .. .. facing p. 765

Camel : What Sinbad Found Out in the Desert .. .. pp. 781–784

Canada : Map of the Dominion of Canada and Newfoundland .. .. .. facing p. 800

Castles that Bid Time Defiance .. .. pp. 857–860

Cathedrals in the English Scene .. .. pp. 869–876

Cave : A Magic Cavern in the Mendip Hills .. .. facing p. 882

Cave : Beauty of Light and Colour in the Blue Grotto .. .. „ „ 883

Cave-dwellers : Cave Drawings of Daily Life 12,000 Years Ago .. .. „ „ 886

Cave-dwellers : How Cave-men Lived in the Far-off Flint Age .. .. .. „ „ 887

Ceylon : Ceylonese Devil-dancer in Full Array .. .. „ „ 904

Ceylon : Gay Tambourine Dancers of Ceylon .. .. „ „ 905

Chameleon Takes his Dinner with his Tongue.. .. .. „ „ 909

Chaucer Rides with the Canterbury Pilgrims .. .. „ „ 929

WHEN YOU ARE IN NEED OF READY REFERENCE

In using THE NEW BOOK OF KNOWLEDGE as a work of reference, Volume Ten is indispensable. As regards its contents that particular volume is unique, for it is at once a complete Index to the preceding Nine Volumes and an Encyclopedia in itself. Its purpose is fourfold, as indicated below.

(1) **Through the Year with the N.B.K.** Its opening section takes the form of a Calendar of the Year, giving for each day all the chief events and matters of interest, with references to the pages of THE NEW BOOK OF KNOWLEDGE in which full particulars concerning the event, personality, or other interest of the day may be found. By the intelligent use of this section (a) the young reader can have the daily delight of reading about topics that have special association with the particular day of the year on which he may be making his reference, (b) father or mother can suggest what would be the most appropriate reading for the day, and (c) the school teacher can set the lessons for the day with a genuine topical appeal.

(2) **Study Outlines.** This large and important section of the volume provides a simple method of study which should enable any of our young readers to become expert in using THE NEW BOOK OF KNOWLEDGE as an auxiliary manual of home study ; and thus what is learnt in school may be amplified and more securely fixed in the memory.

(3) **The Fact-Index.** Actually this is in itself a complete Encyclopedia. In addition to providing many thousands of references to the contents of Volumes One to Nine, it records many more thousands of facts in biography, geography, history, science, the arts, etc., that are not mentioned in its nine predecessors. Therefore, if you look in vain for any subject in the alphabetical order of Volumes One to Nine, turn to Volume Ten and you will almost certainly find it there.

It is a good plan, when using THE NEW BOOK OF KNOWLEDGE as a work of reference, always first to look up any subject in the Fact-Index of Volume Ten.

(4) **Thousands of Additional Entries.** Not only are all the many thousands of statements of fact that appear in the main body of the work carefully recorded in the Fact-Index for your immediate reference, but many thousands of additional entries are given in this exceedingly useful section of our work. By this method the reading pages of the work are saved from the burden of thousands of brief cross-references which the ordinary encyclopedic method would involve. These new entries in the Fact-Index, together with the treasury of reading embodied in Volumes One to Nine, make THE NEW BOOK OF KNOWLEDGE the most comprehensive encyclopedic work produced in the present generation, and assuredly the most readable encyclopedia of its kind.

KEY TO PRONUNCIATION

Most of the subject-headings in THE NEW BOOK OF KNOWLEDGE require no special indication of the way in which they should be pronounced. There are also many for whose proper pronunciation it is only necessary to know which syllable is stressed; in these cases the stress is shown *after* the syllable, thus, A′jax. Where further guidance is necessary, the following signs are employed:

ah = a as in father
aw = a as in ball
ê = vowel sound in fern, word, girl, curl
ow = vowel sound in now, bout
oi = vowel sound in noise, boy
Unmarked vowels have their **short sound**, as a in hat, e in bet, i in bit, o in not, u in but, oo in book
Marked vowels have their **long sound**, as in hāte, bē, bīte, nōte, tūne, bōon

Vowels in italics have a slurred or obscure sound as in abet (*a*-bet′), recent (rē′-s*e*nt), conform (k*o*n-form′), nation (nā′-sh*u*n), tailor (tā′-l*o*r)
th = first sound in thing, thank
th = first sound in the, that
zh = s in measure, leisure
g = hard g, as in good, girl
j = soft g, as in gem, ginger
kh = guttural in loch

LIST OF ABBREVIATIONS

The abbreviations most commonly used in this work are noted below; a much longer list of abbreviations often met with in reading or conversation is given in the Fact-Index that is contained in Volume Ten

A.D., *Anno Domini* (in the year of our Lord, of the Christian era)
a.m., *ante meridiem* (before noon)
b., born
B.C., before Christ
C., Centigrade
c., *circa* (about)
Co., county, company
d., died
e.g., *exempli gratia* (for example)
etc., *et cetera* (and so forth)
et seq., *et sequens* (and following)
F., Fahrenheit
h.p., horse-power

i.e., *id est* (that is)
lb., pound, pounds (weight)
m., miles
MS., MSS., manuscript, manuscripts
oz., ounce, ounces
p.m., *post meridiem* (after noon)
Pop., population
Pron., pronunciation
q.v., *quod vide* (which see)
sq. m., square miles
St., Saint
U.S.A., United States of America
viz., *videlicet* (namely)
yd., yard

The GREATEST BOOK in the WORLD

How the marvellous Jewish and Christian Scriptures have come down to us over more than two thousand years and, though written in ancient tongues and lands far distant, still speak to all in the language of the soul.

Bible. Some 1,200 years ago in a narrow cell in an English monastery the Venerable Bede, the most famous scholar of his day in Western Europe, lay dying. Feebly he dictated his translation of St. John's Gospel, for, although desperately ill he would not rest.

"Go on quickly," he commanded the scribe. "I know not how long I shall hold out or how soon my Master will call me hence." All day long they worked, and when the rays of the setting sun glided into the quiet room, the task was almost done.

"There remains but one chapter, master," said the scribe in anxious tones. "Will you not rest now?"

"Nay, we must go on," Bede replied. "Take up thy pen again and I will translate."

His eyes blinded with tears, the young scribe wrote on. "And now, father," said he, as he set down the last sentence from the quivering lips, "it is finished."

"Ay, it is finished," echoed the dying Bede. And turning his face to the window, he died.

This saintly scholar is only one of the many great men who have spent their lives in making available to all the Bible, the sacred book of Christianity. Translated into Latin, its lessons were the basis of all the church services of the Middle Ages. That its message might be carried to the heathen Teutons and Slavs, Ulfilas devised the Gothic alphabet and Cyril the Slavonic. An English translation of the Bible was the chief treasure of that little band of Puritans who set sail for America to find "freedom to worship God" in their own way. Explorers have carried it into the frozen North and

Oliver Cromwell's pocket Bible, which measures 4½in. by 2½in.

into the heart of the tropical jungles for consolation on their hard journeys; and missionaries, many times at the cost of their lives, have brought its message to heathen lands.

But the Bible is more than our great sacred book; it is also our greatest literary heritage. There is no other book worded with more haunting beauty than our English Bible. Merely as literature it has made a deeper impression upon the human mind than has any other book, and the extent to which it has helped to shape the world's ideas cannot be estimated. No matter how much you may know of poetry and prose, you cannot consider yourself well read unless you have a thoroughly intimate acquaintance with the Bible.

Not One Book but Many

It is a library rather than a book, for it is a collection of 66 books, each distinct in itself, abounding in literature of the highest type. Almost every phase of life and thought is dealt with, and every form of literature is included in its pages—stories, biographies, letters, orations, prayers, hymns of praise, and much else. The beauty and grandeur of some of these books have not been excelled in any other of the sacred writings of the world.

BEDE DICTATING HIS VERSION OF ST. JOHN

The touching scene when the Venerable Bede lay dying, described in this page, is here movingly portrayed in a painting by J. D. Penrose. Bede passed the whole of his life—from the age of seven until his death—in the Benedictine monasteries at Wearmouth and Jarrow in Co. Durham, and he died in Jarrow monastery in 735, at the age of 62.

The Bible has two great divisions, the Old and the New Testament. Testament means "covenant" or mutual understanding—a covenant between God and His people.

The Old Testament is the record of the history and religious literature of a little band of people,

THE CODEX SINAITICUS

In 1933 the British Museum bought the Bible manuscript known as the Codex Sinaiticus for £100,000. Above is Sir George Hill, the Director of the Museum, receiving the MS. from Mr. Maggs, the intermediary in the purchase from the Soviet Government. The Codex, found in a monastery on Mt. Sinai, dates from the 4th century A.D., and is written in Greek, as is seen from the extract in the lower picture.

PSALM ON PAPYRUS

One of the earliest existing manuscripts of any part of the Bible is a papyrus now in the British Museum, a portion of which is shown above. It contains a translation of the Twelfth Psalm from Hebrew into Greek. Much of it has perished, but even such a fragment as this is highly prized by scholars.
Trustees of British Museum

the Jews, who believed in one God who was loving and just. All about the little country of Palestine were great and powerful nations, who worshipped many gods, but Israel managed to retain its belief in only one God. In the New Testament is the story of the life of Jesus and His teachings, and the acts and epistles (letters) of the Apostles. All through the Old Testament are promises that God would give His people a deliverer; and these promises, which Christianity teaches were fulfilled in the life and death of Jesus, give the thread of unity binding the Old Testament to the New.

The Old Testament as we know it is by no means the whole of the sacred writings of the Jewish people. It was not until 200 years after Christianity had been founded that the rabbis and teachers of the Jews finally decided which of their books should be regarded as "canonical" in the Jewish Church. "Canon" means literally a rule or measure, and, applied to the Bible, it means a list of books which were accepted as inspired. These " canonical scriptures " of the Jews became the Old Testament of the Christians. But the early Christian Church put 14 of the rejected books in a separate group at the end of the Old Testament. These we call the *Apocrypha*—which is the Greek word for " hidden," or the " hidden books."

The Roman Catholic Church still uses these Apocryphal books. They include the books of Tobit, Judith, the remainder of Esther, the remainder of Daniel, the Wisdom of Solomon, Ecclesiasticus (called " The Wisdom of Jesus, the son of Sirach "), Baruch, Maccabees 1 and 2. All the leading English translations down to the King James Version included these books, and the scholars who gave us the Revised Version revised these books with the rest, although they were published in a separate volume. Some of the passages are equal in nobility of thought and language to passages from the books included as inspired.

Similarly, there was for a long time a difference of opinion as to what books should be included in the New Testament. There are no less than 109 of the New Testament Apocryphal books, whose very names are unfamiliar to most Christians today ; examples are the Epistle of Barnabas, the Teaching of the Twelve Apostles, and the Shepherd of Hermas. The canon of the New Testament was not decided until A.D. 382 at a council held at Rome.

The oldest manuscripts of the collected books of the Bible go back only to about A.D. 350. There are only a few of these. The oldest one, known as the Codex Vaticanus, is kept in the Vatican Library at Rome ; it contains almost the whole of the New Testament.

The Sinaitic manuscript, discovered in St. Catherine's monastery at the foot of Mt. Sinai in 1844, was purchased from Russia by Britain in 1933. It probably dates from the early part of the fourth century. The Alexandrine manuscript, written after A.D. 400, was presented to King Charles I of England and is now in the British Museum ; it contains the greater part of both the Old and New Testa-

ments. Some of these old manuscripts are called " palimpsests " (from Greek terms meaning to rub away again), the original writing on the parchment sheets being erased to make room for later writing. Means have been found, however, to restore the old letters, so that they show up faintly.

The New Testament was written in Greek. There are nearly 2,000 ancient manuscripts of the whole or different parts of the New Testament written in this language, but none is older than the manuscripts described above. In the past 30 years, however, in excavations made in Egypt, there have been found several pages containing " sayings of Jesus," which are probably a full century or more older than the oldest New Testament manuscripts we have.

The work of comparing such early manuscripts and correcting the text and revising the translation has gone on from early days. When the Temple at Jerusalem was burned in A.D. 70 much of the sacred literature of the Jews was lost ; but a school of rabbis was

THE BIBLE IS BROUGHT TO THE PEOPLE

For centuries the common people were deliberately kept in ignorance of the book on which their religion rested, and it was not until the first great English reformer, John Wycliffe, translated the Latin version into English in 1382 that they were allowed to realize all that it meant to them. In this painting, by W. F. Yeames, R.A., Wycliffe is seen sending out his wandering disciples, each with a hand-written copy of the Bible.

formed at Tiberias to restore it. Alexandria in Egypt early became a centre for the study of the Christian writings. All through the Middle Ages patient monks busied themselves with the labour of copying and so preserving the sacred texts. And with the publication of the printed Greek text of the New Testament by Erasmus in 1516 the modern study of the Bible began.

The Old Testament was written in Hebrew (except for a few passages in the Aramaic dialect),

READING THE BIBLE IN OLD ST. PAUL'S

When the majority of people in England were illiterate, and, moreover, the cost of the book was very high, many could get to know the Bible story only by listening to a scholar reading to them in church. Here a nineteenth-century artist, Sir George Harvey, has painted such a scene in Old St. Paul's Cathedral in London. You will notice that the precious Book is chained to the pillar.

people of his time could understand them. (*See* Caedmon). Other translators, including Bede, gave the people of England fragments of the scriptures in their own tongue, but it was not until the year 1382 that the whole Bible was translated into English.

This first English Bible, translated from the Latin Vulgate (1382) and copied out by hand, is considered by many to be the work of the group of early reformers headed by John Wycliffe, and bears his name. Great opposition arose to it because its authors translated many passages in a sense not approved by the Church. Nevertheless, it was so widely circulated that, in spite of the fact that its reading was prohibited by law, there are more than 100 manuscript copies of it preserved today.

and the New Testament in a popular form of Greek and in Aramaic. The Old Testament was translated into Greek about 270 B.C. by a committee of seventy. Their version is known as the Septuagint, from the Latin word meaning " seventy." In every country where Christianity spread, the Bible was translated into the language of that country—first into various eastern dialects, then into Latin, the language of the Romans, and then into the languages of Western Europe. No other book has been translated into so many languages.

The greatest of the early translations was that into Latin made by St. Jerome, who lived about 400 years after Christ. This translation, known as the Vulgate, is today the official Bible of the Roman Catholic Church throughout the world. It was also the basis of the earlier translations into English and other European tongues and of the Douai English translation which is used by English-speaking Catholics. It is a wonderful testimony to the interest taken in the Bible that when printing was invented in the 15th century, the Latin Bible was the first complete book printed.

Parts of the Bible were early translated into English. The first writer to do this was Caedmon, though it is true he did not translate the Bible at all in the usual sense, but sang its divine stories so that the ignorant

WILLIAM TYNDALE : TRANSLATOR AND MARTYR

So strong was the Church's and State's objection to the people learning the true foundations of the Bible by reading its words in their own tongue that Tyndale, its second great English translator, was strangled and burned as a heretic. In this well-known painting by A. Johnstone, William Tyndale (the seated figure) is shown working at his glorious task.

William Tyndale, who was born a hundred years after Wycliffe's death, went back to the original Hebrew and Greek versions, and his translation of many passages is so good that much of it is preserved in the English Bible of the present time. But Tyndale, too, was a "heretic," and when his books first reached England from the Continent they were burned as "pernicious merchandise." The new art of printing, however, spread his Bible far and wide. In the end Tyndale was condemned as a heretic on the Continent, being strangled and burned at the stake in Belgium in 1536.

Miles Coverdale's Bible (authorized in 1535) was founded in part on Tyndale's translation ; while the "Great Bible," ordered by Henry VIII in 1539 to be placed in all the churches, was partly based on Coverdale and partly on the work of John Rogers, later a martyr. A revision of the Great Bible was issued in 1568 ; it was known as the Bishops' Bible.

When James I came to the throne, the Reformation had been accomplished in Great Britain and the church services were all in English. He desired an English Bible more perfect than any then existing, so he instructed 47 Biblical scholars to prepare a new translation. They were divided into small companies, each company translating a book or several books of the Bible. They kept the earlier versions, especially that of Tyndale, before them, so that there are whole sentences in their version which are the same as in earlier translations. The result of their labours was the King James Version, published in 1611, which has been for over 300 years the "Authorized Version" of the Protestant English-speaking people. It is the greatest book in the English language. "Its simple, majestic, Anglo-Saxon tongue," says one writer, "its clear, sparkling style, its directness and force of utterance, have made it the model in language, style and dignity of some of the choicest writers of the last two centuries, and its reverential and spiritual tone and attitude have made it

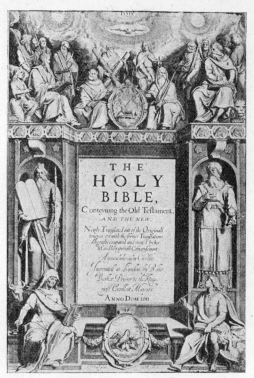

'KING JAMES'S BIBLE'

It was King James I who ordered the preparation of our great "Authorized Version" of the Bible, which has been and still remains the finest literary treasure of our language. Here is the title page of the first edition of the book, completed, by nearly half a hundred scholars, in 1611.

the idol of the Christian Church and endeared it to the hearts of millions."

It may be noted that its language is not that of the early 17th century, but of the Tudor Age, for the translators depended very largely on the Bishops' Bible, which in turn was based on Tyndale's.

For English-speaking Catholics, a similar place is held by the Douai Version. This was first produced at the University of Douai, in France, by Catholic refugees from England in Elizabeth's day. Dr. Gregory Martin, formerly of Oxford, played the chief part in the translation, which was revised by William Allen and others. The New Testament was published in 1582, and the whole Bible in two volumes in 1609 and 1610.

The Revised Version, made desirable by the discovery of new manuscripts, was published in 1881 by a committee of English scholars co-operating with a similar committee appointed in the United States. Its translations are more accurate, but it lacks the beauty of language of the King James (or Authorized) Version.

A number of further revisions have been made in an attempt not only to render the original more accurately but to express it in more modern speech. Thus we have Dr. R. F. Weymouth's "New Testament in Modern Speech"; the Moffatt Bible, translated by Rev. James Moffatt; the "Twentieth Century New Testament"; and translations of certain books of the Bible under the auspices of the Adult School Union.

There have been many editions of the Bible possessing some feature of particular interest. Among the more remarkable we may mention :

The "Mazarin Bible" was the first complete book printed from movable types (1452–56). It is so named because the first copy discovered was found among the books of Cardinal Mazarin.

The "Complutensian Polyglot," published by Cardinal Ximenes in 1522, prints the Greek of the New Testament in one column and the Latin of the Vulgate in the other. For the

Old Testament it gives the Hebrew on one side and the old Greek translation (called the Septuagint) on the other, and the Latin Vulgate between—" like Christ crucified between the two thieves," so the preface says.

The " Bug Bible " (1551) was so called because of the translation of Psalm xci, 5, which read, " afraid of bugs by night," instead of the present " terror by night."

The " Breeches Bible " is an English version published at Geneva in 1560, and is named from its translation of Gen. iii, 7, which reads, "making themselves *breeches* out of fig leaves."

The " Wicked Bible," printed in England in 1631, left out the word " not " in the Seventh Commandment.

The " Thumb Bible," published in 1670 at Aberdeen, was one inch square and one-half inch thick.

ONE OF THE SMALLEST BIBLES

This is the little Bible referred to in this page. Made in Glasgow in 1901, it is so small that it may be slipped into a waistcoat pocket. Yet there are other Bibles which are almost too heavy to lift !

The " Vinegar Bible " (1717) has as the heading of the 20th chapter of Luke "The Parable of the Vinegar," instead of " vineyard."

The " Devil's Bible " is the name given to a manuscript of the Bible taken to Stockholm after the Thirty Years' War. It is beautifully written on 300 asses' skins, and legend says it is the work of a monk condemned to death, who by selling himself to Satan was enabled to save his life by meeting the condition that he should copy the whole Bible on asses' skins in one night.

One of the smallest Bibles in the world was printed in Glasgow in 1901. Without the cover it is 1¼ by 1¾ inches, and seven-sixteenths of an inch thick, containing 876 pages and several illustrations. It is provided with a small magnifying glass which slips into a pocket in the cover.

Bibliography. (Pron. bib-li-og'-rafi).

There are said to exist in printed form about eight and a half million separate writings, each long enough to be called a book. No one can, of course, read more than a few thousand of them in the course of his lifetime. It is, therefore, important that he select for his reading the books which will best serve his particular needs. Bibliography is the science which has been designed to assist him in making his selection.

The word comes from two Greek words meaning " book " and " writing." Thus in the broadest sense any literary composition about books might be called a bibliography. In ordinary use, however, the word has a narrower meaning, being usually applied only to instructive lists of books, concerned with special subjects or branches of subjects.

Necessarily, there are all sorts of bibliographies to meet all sorts of different needs. There are author bibliographies, as, for example, a list of all the writings of Charles Dickens ; subject bibliographies, such as lists of useful books about chemistry ; bibliographies of literary form, like lists of one-act plays ; local bibliographies, such as a list of the works dealing with Kent or Wessex ; period bibliographies, like lists of the literary productions of the Age of Elizabeth ; language bibliographies, as a list of books written in Spanish. There are even bibliographies of bibliographies.

For the convenience of the reader, a good bibliography distributes its subjects under logical subdivisions. A bibliography should divide and subdivide its subjects until only a few books are included under each topic, and arrange these topics so logically that a reader can turn quickly to the particular section he wants.

The bibliographer must also be accurate. When he mentions a book he must do so in such a way that his reader can be certain of just what book he means. To achieve this he will do well to use the conventional system which has proved well suited for the purpose. This system records certain facts about each book which may be regarded as the indispensable elements of detailed bibliographical description. In their simplest form these are : author, title, place of publication, date of publication, and size of the book. All except the last of these elements appear on the title page of every ordinary book.

In the record of size conventional usage varies. Usually approximate indications are sufficient. It makes little difference to the ordinary reader whether a book contains 272 or 288 pages, but it makes a great difference whether it is a slender pamphlet or an extensive treatise in many volumes. Similarly, most readers will want to know whether a book is a portable volume or the size of an encyclopedia.

Every librarian, by the very nature of his profession, must be something of a bibliographer. Students who wish to pursue the study of any special subject should, therefore, approach a librarian and ask him to make out a list of books on that subject. It is one of the great benefits of the science of bibliography that a librarian can do this without being an expert on the subject in question.

Bihar. A province of British India west of Bengal and bordered on the north by Nepal, Bihar, until the Government of India Act came into force in April 1937, was joined administratively to Orissa. It is now a separate province, with an area of 69,348 sq. miles and a population of over 32,000,000, chiefly engaged in agriculture. Owing to the density of the population Bihar formerly suffered severely from famine, but an increase of railway and canal transport has averted such disasters.

In the district of Chota Nagpur there are large deposits of coal yielding 12,000,000 tons annually out of British India's total output of 18,000,000 tons. At Jamshedpur in the south of Bihar (population 83,000) are the famous Tata Iron and Steel Works employing 27,000 hands. Mica is also produced, and about 120,000 persons are employed in the coal, iron ore and mica mines. The East Indian, Bengal and North Western, Bengal Nagpur and Eastern Bengal Railways traverse the province. Nine million acres are devoted to the cultivation of rice, while maize, oilseeds, wheat and barley are also grown. The capital, Patna, on the Ganges, has a population of 158,000, and other important towns are Gaya (88,000) and Bhagalpur (83,000). Near Gaya is Buddh Gaya, where Buddha sat beneath the sacred bo-tree and became "enlightened." The Government is moved to Ranchi, in the hills, during the hot weather.

Bilberry. There are two names for this plant (*Vaccinium myrtillus*). In some parts of the country it is called the blaeberry and in others the whortleberry. It is a low shrub about the same height as heather, to which it is related, and grows in similar places, that is, on heaths and hills. It is usually found in great quantities, hiding the ground with a dense covering of small oval, tough, leathery leaves ; in some localities it makes such a carpet under oak trees or other woodland.

In spring it has a beautiful little flower, which looks like a tiny pinky-white inverted globe. But the plant is seldom noticed except in autumn, and then its attraction is its delicious little round berry, which is covered with a most tempting blue bloom like that of the sloe and which makes a delicious jam.

Billiards. This game has been played in many different ways at various times, and even today there is a marked difference between the English, French and American styles, but in

H. Bastin

BILBERRY IN FLOWER

The humble bilberry is not a very noticeable or attractive plant, and you would probably not see it among the heather when it is not flowering or fruiting. But in blossom time it bears pretty little pinkish balls, later to be followed by the tasty bluish berries that give it its name.

whatever style it is played, it requires a steadiness of touch and an accuracy of eye such as no other game needs.

The full-sized table is twelve feet long and six feet wide, and has a perfectly level green baize surface surrounded by a bevelled rail of rubber cushions. Pockets are placed at the four corners, and one in the centre of each side.

The game is played by two players, each of whom has a cue, which is a wooden rod generally about five feet long, and varying in diameter from half an inch or less at the point to an inch and a half at the butt. Upon the point is fixed a leather tip. Three balls are used, two being white and one red, one of the white balls having a black spot. Hence one player is " spot " and the other " plain."

This diagram shows the markings used in the games of billiards, pyramids and snooker.

Scores are made by cannons, winning hazards and losing hazards. A cannon is scored when the striker's ball hits the other two, a losing hazard when it enters a pocket after hitting either. A winning hazard is scored when either the red or white ball is " potted " or sent into a pocket by the striker's ball. A cannon

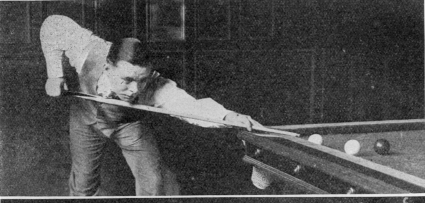

MASTERS OF THE BILLIARDS TABLE

The greatest modern exponent of billiards is undoubtedly Walter Lindrum, an Australian (lower picture.) Above is Joe Davis, an outstanding English player. Both are making easy cannon shots, which will score two points each.

is the Declaration of the Rights of Man issued by the French Assembly at the time of the French Revolution in 1789. It laid down the principles of the freedom and equality under the law of all citizens and the sovereignty of the people, as well as the rights of the individual to freedom of speech, of religion, and of the press. It has well been said that it "laid down the principles of modern governments." This declaration passed beyond the frontiers of France and became an important factor in the growth of democracy in the 19th century.

Biochemistry.

The most marvellous chemical laboratory is the body of a living creature. In the countless tiny cells of every plant or animal, chemical changes are constantly taking place, so wonderful and complex that they are at once the joy and the despair of the chemist. The study of the processes going on day and night in the microscopic cells that make up the various tissues—bone, muscle, blood, glands, etc.—is one of the newest and most fascinating fields into which chemistry has entered. It is called biochemistry, or the science of living matter.

The first step in studying the chemistry of life is a knowledge of the nature of protoplasm, the substance of which all living things are made. Twelve chemical elements may be said to be indispensable to protoplasm : carbon, hydrogen, oxygen, nitrogen, phosphorus, sulphur, sodium, chlorine, magnesium, iron, potassium and calcium. In plant physiology additional elements, e.g. silicon, iodine and bromide, are found intimately associated with protoplasm. These chemical elements combine to form the four great groups of organic compounds : proteins, carbohydrates, fats and lipoids, as well as enzymes, inorganic salts and water.

Proteins are complex compounds of carbon, hydrogen, oxygen and nitrogen. Nearly all contain traces also of sulphur and phosphorus, and sometimes of magnesium and iron. The

counts two ; a winning or losing hazard off white ball two, and off red ball three. A player continues his " break " until he fails to score.

Also played on a billiard table is the game known as snooker pool, now very popular. It is played with 22 balls, 15 of which are red, and the others of various colours and values. Winning hazards are the only means of scoring in snooker, cannons being ignored.

Bill of Rights.

After Magna Carta the great bulwark of English liberty is the Bill of Rights passed by the English Parliament in 1689, after William and Mary had been brought to the throne by the Revolution of 1688. It drew attention to the unconstitutional conduct of James II, and contained a number of clauses to protect the freedom of the people. Thus it guaranteed a fair trial in the courts, frequent meetings of Parliament and freedom of debate therein, freedom from taxation except by Parliament, the right of petition, etc. Several of the first ten amendments to the constitution of the United States, including the one forbidding " excessive bail " and " cruel and unusual punishments," are taken from the Bill.

The most important statement of rights which the State may not take from the individual protein molecule is very large. Casein, for instance, the characteristic protein of milk, has a formula like $C_{708}H_{1130}O_{224}N_{180}S_4P_4$. How different this is from the simple formula for water, H_2O! The structural units of the protein molecule are known as amino acids, which are organic acids containing nitrogen. All proteins contain nitrogen and are often described as the nitrogenous substances of food. So important are amino acids that they have been called the building stones of life. They determine rate of growth, rate of body weight production and of skeletal development. The fibrin found in clotted blood, the myosin of muscles, and the gelatin of bones are examples of protein. (*See* Proteins).

Carbohydrates, as the name indicates, are compounds of carbon, hydrogen and oxygen. They comprise starches, sugars, cellulose, gums, and many other substances. Carbohydrates combine readily with oxygen and serve as the fundamental sources of energy in living things.

Fats and *lipoids* are organic compounds greasy to the touch and capable of being dissolved in ether, alcohol and chloroform. Fats are composed of the same chemical elements as the carbohydrates, but contain much less oxygen in proportion to the carbon. Butter, lard and olive oil are examples of fats (*see* Fats and Oils). Lipoids are similar to fats, but contain phosphorus and nitrogen, or nitrogen only, in addition to carbon, hydrogen and oxygen.

Enzymes are organic substances, mostly of unknown chemical composition, which play the part of catalysts in life processes. Catalysts are agents that bring about or hasten a chemical reaction without appearing among the final products of the reaction and without being themselves changed chemically. All cells produce enzymes, but some, the gland cells, specialize in this production and give forth enzymes to take part in external reactions, as in digestion. The *inorganic salts* contained in protoplasm

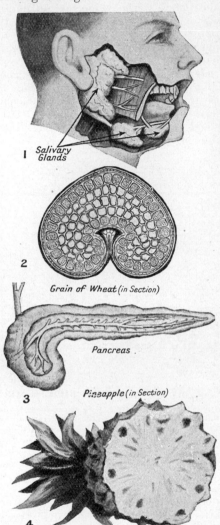

1 Salivary Glands

2 Grain of Wheat *(in Section)*

Pancreas

3 Pineapple *(in Section)*

4

DIGESTIVE FERMENTS

Above are (1) human salivary glands, which secrete ptyalin, a ferment or enzyme that converts sugar into starch; (2) wheat grain, containing a similar ferment; (3) human pancreas, secreting trypsin; and (4) pineapple, which contains a like enzyme.

are chiefly sodium and calcium chloride, with other minerals like potassium and magnesium found in sea water. These salts are held in crystalline solution by water, which constitutes 60 to 90 per cent of protoplasm. Physically, protoplasm is a colloidal system, and the watery solution acts as the dispersion medium for the finely-divided proteins, carbohydrates, fats and lipoids.

Knowledge of the chemical structure of protoplasm is essential for the understanding of metabolism, a general term for the chemical changes taking place in the cell. Obviously, proper food for an organism must contain the elements or compounds found in its cell protoplasm and, in addition, it must have those substances called vitamins. (*See* Food; Vitamins).

Biochemistry deals with the processes by which food, when it has been fully digested, is assimilated into the tissue cells of the organism to become cellular protoplasm. This part of metabolism is called catabolism.

Metabolism also includes those reactions by which the constituents of protoplasm are chemically decomposed for the transformation of energy and the production of heat. This destructive part of metabolism is known as anabolism. These activities are really oxidations, that is, reactions in which oxygen unites with compounds of the protoplasmic system. Oxidations provide heat and energy for doing work; they furnish the power for the living machine. (*See* Oxygen).

In vertebrate animals the oxygen is carried by *haemoglobin*, an iron compound found in the red blood cells. Combined with haemoglobin, oxygen is distributed throughout the body by the blood stream as *oxyhaemoglobin*, a very unstable combination which allows free oxygen to be promptly released to the body cells when the blood enters the capillaries.

Within the cells there is a pigment called *cytochrome*, which takes hold of the oxygen and controls it in the narrow confines of the cell laboratory. Oxygen, the workman, is now on the job. Cytochrome, the foreman, holds it there. But atmospheric oxygen is sluggish, it acts too slowly, it must in some manner be "activated." The cell is ready for this emergency with oxidizing enzymes, which hasten the union of oxygen and assimilated foods.

The process of oxidation in living tissues is identical with ordinary combustion. Carbohydrates and fats are completely oxidized in the body and are the chief sources of animal energy, some of which is converted into heat. Proteins are also oxidized to a slight extent. The living fire consumes fuel, creates heat, but also leaves behind waste products of combustion. The oxidation of carbohydrates, fats and lipoids gives rise to carbon dioxide and water. In the case of proteins the end products of combustion are carbon dioxide, water and a

getting enough oxygen to burn up the lactic acid which has accumulated in his blood and tissues. In a short time his muscles are recharged with glycogen and he is ready for another race.

Other interesting problems from the biochemical standpoint are growth, which is increase in size, and reproduction, which is increase in numbers. Both of these life functions are under the control of internal secretions or hormones. The formation of the hormones by various organs of the body is primarily a chemical process, and their use by the body also involves chemical problems.

Turning now to the study of plants, we find similar problems of great importance for the biochemist. By far the most important chemical reaction taking place on earth is *photosynthesis*. This is the process which occurs in plants, when, in the presence of sunlight and a pigment called chlorophyll, carbon dioxide and water unite to form carbohydrates, and oxygen is evolved as a by-product. (*See* Leaves; Plant Life). All life depends upon this process, for it makes a source of energy available to both plants and animals. It is the reaction by which organic foods are made out of inorganic materials.

PRACTICAL EXPERIMENT BY A PIONEER BIOCHEMIST

A. L. Lavoisier (1743-1794), the great French chemist, was the first to demonstrate the difference between inspired and expired air. That difference, we now know, is represented by carbon dioxide (CO_2), the poisonous waste of the body got rid of by breathing. This sketch, by his wife, seen on the right, shows Lavoisier conducting the actual experiment.

variety of nitrogen-containing compounds. These products are no longer of use to the body. They are the waste materials of metabolism, which are dealt with by the excretory system.

Another aspect of living matter is its ability to perform movements. Animal movements are due to the shortening or contracting of muscle fibres. How is this brought about? When a nerve-message "orders" a muscle to contract, glycogen, or "animal starch" present in the muscle fibres, is changed into an intermediary substance which gives rise to lactic acid. The lactic acid by its mere presence causes the fibres to contract, and work is done. But if the muscle is to recover and do more work, the lactic acid has to be removed. Part of it is changed into glycogen again; the remainder forms carbon dioxide and water. In this recovery phase oxygen is essential. An athlete, panting after a race, is unconsciously

Once the plant is supplied with carbohydrates, it can proceed to the manufacture of proteins, fats, acids, alkaloids, etc., obtaining for this purpose the necessary mineral matter from the soil.

Think of all the useful products that are built up in the biochemical laboratory of the plant! Not only foods for man and animal, but gums, camphors, resins, all the varieties of oils and essences, rubber, alcohol, tannin, iodine, the drugs that cure our ills, quinine, atropine, and a wealth of other substances. Photosynthesis is behind all this; and plants produce oxygen, a constant supply of which is essential if we are to breathe.

Let us glance for a moment at some of the methods which chemists use in attacking life problems. The chemist begins by taking apart, or analysing, materials whose transformations he wishes to understand. He sorts out the various ingredients. He attempts to isolate pure principles from a complex mixture.

So he discovers cocaine, or insulin, or thyroxin. Then he attempts to resolve such compounds into their chemical elements. Not satisfied with this, he considers the groupings of atoms in the molecule—the smallest particle of the substance. He tries to picture the way in which these atoms are linked together. This enables him in many cases to prepare the product artificially and more cheaply.

For example, cocaine, the first drug used to produce local anaesthesia, has serious drawbacks. It occurs in the leaves of the coca plant, and, because rare, is expensive. Moreover, it is dangerous and habit-forming. The discovery of the exact molecular structure of cocaine led to the artificial preparation of a similar compound called procaine (or novocaine), which is just as effective as cocaine without being dangerous or habit-forming. Novocaine, together perhaps with adrenalin, another drug made usable by the work of the organic chemist, is what your dentist probably uses when he gives you an injection.

This, then, is the hope of the biochemist : to understand the chemical structure of life substances, to gain a knowledge of life's chemical processes, and then to imitate, control, or improve upon Nature's methods for the benefit of mankind.

Biography AND AUTOBIOGRAPHY. A book that relates a man's or woman's life-story is called a biography, and when a person tries to set forth his own life in a book it is known as an autobiography. There are, of course, innumerable examples of both classes.

Biography is a useful handmaid to history, and there is no better way really to understand any period than to study the lives of people who lived during that period. There could, for example, be no pleasanter approach to an understanding of the men and movements that led to Italian unity than through Trevelyan's three great works on Garibaldi.

One of the earliest biographies is that in which the Latin writer, Tacitus, describes the life of his father-in-law, Agricola, a famous soldier who fought and conquered in Britain. The Greek writer, Plutarch, also left a collection of biographies, numbering nearly fifty ; and from these, in an English translation, Shakespeare drew many of the incidents and characters in his great tragedies.

Biography has flourished in more recent times, and in our own language. Boswell's " Life of Johnson " is one of the greatest books in English, and is by some regarded as the greatest biography ever written. Others prefer Lockhart's " Life of Scott." Dr. Johnson himself wrote several biographies, which were published as " Lives of the Poets," and the famous writer, Thomas Carlyle, devoted many laborious years to writing the lives of Oliver Cromwell and Frederick the Great, and the life of Thomas Carlyle has in turn been described by a dozen writers since his death—notably by James Anthony Froude, a friend of Carlyle, whose biography of him aroused a storm of controversy, and David Alec Wilson, who for forty years collected material of all kinds about Carlyle.

There has been a spate of biographies during the last twenty years, many of them written in a critical and cynical spirit, sometimes disparaging instead of praising the people with whom they deal. This new method of biography is generally regarded as originating with Lytton Strachey, who employed it effectively in his " Eminent Victorians " (1918). Lytton Strachey's books were always the product of wide reading and research, so that, while his interpretations are often original, they are founded upon a deep knowledge of facts. Those who have tried to copy his style have not always imitated his industry and accuracy.

Autobiography was not practised as a form of literature by the writers of ancient Greece and Rome. But the spread of the Christian religion, which encouraged people to consider more carefully their own thoughts and actions, gave a stimulus to the writing of autobiographies. Thus in the fourth century A.D. St. Augustine wrote his " Confessions," telling of his life, his inward struggles, and his final conversion to Christianity. This book was very popular throughout the Middle Ages, and inspired a great many people to write their lives as Augustine had done.

In the eighteenth century the Frenchman, Jean-Jacques Rousseau, wrote his "Confessions," which, when they were published after his death, created a great and lasting impression.

Several great authors have written their autobiographies, among others Leigh Hunt, Gibbon, James Hogg, William Cobbett, Anthony Trollope, and Edward John Trelawny. That of Trelawny, " Adventures of a Younger Son," is, perhaps, the most thrilling to read.

Autobiographies of the Present Day

Of recent years the autobiography has become very common, until today it is almost taken for granted that anyone who has reached eminence will write a book about himself or herself. Among recent autobiographies may be mentioned those of Winston Churchill, David Lloyd George and George Lansbury among politicians, those of H. G. Wells, Frank Swinnerton and Laurence Housman among authors, of Dame Ethel Smyth among musicians, and of Sir John Martin Harvey, Sir Frank Benson and Sir Henry Lytton among actors.

MARVELS *of the* SCIENCE *of* LIFE

Below are presented the chief facts of Biology, the science which teaches the "oneness" of Life throughout all its more than 2,000,000 forms— worms and fishes, apes and men, trees, mushrooms and seaweed!

Biology. This, in brief, is "the science of life." There are at least two million kinds of living things in the world. With all

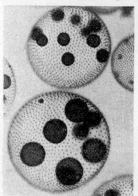

their irreconcilable contrasts—men, earth-worms, jelly-fishes, oak trees, ferns, seaweeds —they yet possess one feature in common: life. And so we have the common great science of biology, which deals especially with the far-reaching fundamental characters of living things.

Of course, this study is so vast that it is impossible for any one man to cover or master the whole field in detail. Consequently, it is broken up into divisions, of which the primary ones are botany, the science of plant life, and zoology, the science of animal life ; and each natural scientist further specializes in some narrower line, such as anatomy, physiology, embryology, genetics, or some other of a large number of such fields. But there is still place for the general science of biology, to take account of living things especially in their larger relations, and to correlate all of the many divisions of the subject.

The modern science of biology differs from the old-time "natural history" chiefly in that the latter was, in the main, a great accumulation of disconnected facts about plants and animals. Biology, on the other hand, takes account of the detailed facts mainly as they illustrate the principles and laws that govern life. At present the term natural history is customarily applied especially to the out-of-doors study of the habitats, habits, modes of life, seasons, and activities of living things, both plants and animals. While this outside study of living things has its wonderful fascinations, the same is true also of the other phases of

their study ; but these take more patience, serious study, and often the use of the microscope and other facilities.

Common forms of life, of course, are easily divided into the two great types—plants and animals—with clear distinguishing characters for each. At the bottom of the scale of life, however, the plant and animal kingdoms converge, and there are some simple microscopic forms which are not clearly one or the other, but possess some characters of each. And so it is impossible to draw a sharp line between the plant and animal kingdoms. But between clear-cut plants and animals, the following are the main differences.

Green plants are able, in the presence of sunlight, by means of their green chlorophyll, to utilize salts and water drawn from the soil, and carbonic acid obtained from the air, in building up their own substance. This cannot be done by Man artificially, or by animals naturally. In this way green plants furnish the fundamental food supply, not only for all animal life in the world, but also for the colour-less fungus plants such as mushrooms and moulds. In this wonderful work the green chlorophyll is the "machine" that does the work ; the sun's rays furnish the radiant energy that is transformed into chemically stored energy in the form of starch, sugar and the other energy-yielding foods of Man and all other animals. The cells of plants have walls of woody material; animals have not. Plants are usually stationary ; most animals move freely.

But with all these differences, it still remains true that both types of living things possess the main fundamental characters of life in common. In all organisms, the living substance is protoplasm. (*See* Protoplasm.) And while there must be infinite variety of tissue, as found in different plants and animals and in different parts of the same plant or the same animal, protoplasm is the same fundamentally everywhere. It is made up of some or all of the same 12 elements (carbon,

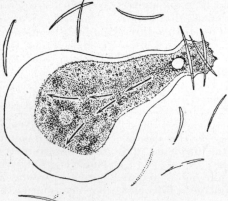

LIFE AT ITS SIMPLEST
Here, enormously magnified, is a single-celled amoeba—the simplest form of animal life. When the outer transparent layer contracts, the inner mass of protoplasm is forced in the direction of the arrows. Top left, Volvox globator, also greatly magnified, represents the next rung in life's ladder.

THE MOST WONDERFUL OF ALL LIFE'S PROCESSES

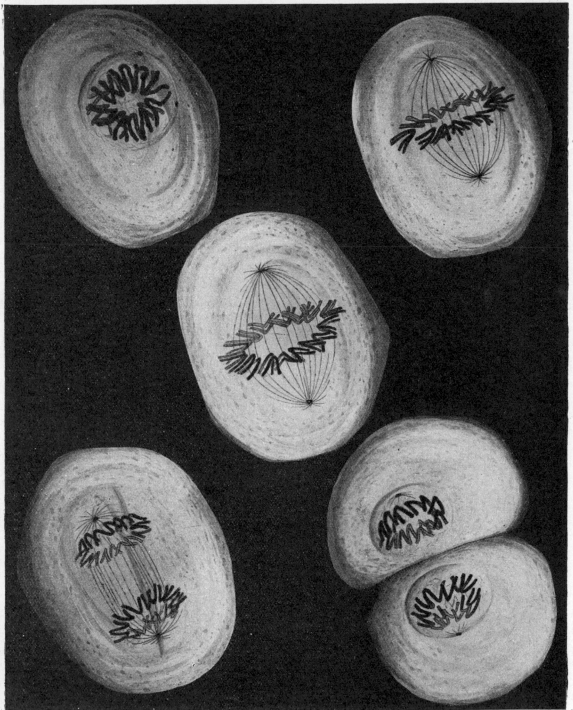

Here you see Nature's way of developing a new life from a fertilized egg. In the upper left-hand corner is a cell, enormously magnified. The sphere in the centre is the "nucleus." Those black rods shaped like bent pins inside the nucleus are "chromosomes." They are made up of the wonderful substance called "chromatin," half of which comes from the mother and half from the father. On the edge of the nucleus are two black specks called "centrosomes." This first cell shows us the very beginning of life. Now watch that tiny life grow! In the upper right-hand corner the centrosomes have separated to opposite poles and a delicate arrangement of fibres has been formed to which the chromosomes have attached themselves. The cell in the centre shows the most wonderful stage of all, for it tells us the secret of heredity. See how each of the chromosome rods has split lengthwise into exactly equal halves! In the next cell at the left, half of each rod has been pulled away from the other half by those centrosome fibres, forming now two separate groups, each made up of mother and father elements alike. In the last picture the cell walls have split, forming two new cells like the first. These will in turn split into two, and so again and again, and the new life will grow to become a plant, or a fish, or an elephant, or a man, depending upon the nature of the parent chromatin.

oxygen, nitrogen, hydrogen, sulphur, calcium, potassium, magnesium, iron, phosphorus, chlorine and sodium), and contains none that is not common in Nature everywhere. Protoplasm possesses everywhere the same general physiology ; is sensitive to external conditions, such as touch, temperature, chemical, etc ; there is some form of response, especially apparent in the motion of animals. All organisms utilize food and grow ; possess respiration, the taking in of oxygen and giving off of carbonic acid ; and reproduce their kind by some form of reproduction. One of the most extraordinary and important resemblances is the striking and intricate method of cell division described in the chapter on Cell.

In viewing the life of the world, it is always fascinating to think of the combination of the great number of conditions that are necessary to make life possible on earth—all of them necessary. First, there is the sun, the sole source of all the energy for plant growth and for the food supply for the whole living world, as well as of light and heat. And so it was, through the many million years of the infinite past, while Nature was slowly and patiently depositing the vast storehouses of energy in the form of coal, oil and gas, for the uses of modern Man—all derived from the remains of the plants and animals of the past ! Vast quantities of water are also absolutely necessary. Water forms the larger part of protoplasm and is the universal solvent for the foods of both plants and animals. The water vapour of the atmosphere furnishes a blanket that helps to retain the heat from the sun. The vast reservoirs of the sea help to stabilize the temperature of the earth. An atmosphere of moderate temperature, with oxygen for respiration for all life and with carbonic acid for plant food, is absolutely necessary, as are also all of the chemical elements that enter into the formation of protoplasm. There are yet other conditions, more difficult to explain.

Space will permit but a few broad considerations of the distribution and interrelations of living things in the world. In general, the variety and wealth of plant life is on land, of animal life in the sea.

All are familiar with the general conditions of life in the field and woods. The liberal

vegetation, mostly of flowering plants, furnishes the fundamental food supply for animal life—insects, birds, mice, rabbits. Even where predacious animals feed on other animals, the latter have fed on plants. The interrelations —" the web of life "—are extremely intricate. And so it is, in greatly magnified degree, in the tropical forest. One thinks there of the luxuriant dense matted vegetation, sheltering its teeming life of insects and tropical birds and other strange life of the jungle. Here the

THE STORY OF THE TRANSMISSION OF LIFE

TO understand how life—animal or vegetable, minute or gigantic—is constituted, you must first grasp the essential fact that all life is made up of tiny units of protoplasm which we call "cells." These cells are of many kinds, each with a special task to perform. There are blood cells to carry oxygen from the lungs to all parts of the body, muscle cells for movement, gland cells to produce digestive juices, nerve cells to convey messages back and forth. But all of them have come from a single cell. By a beautiful and mysterious process this single cell divides into two, and each of these into two—always two—and so on, until there have been formed the millions and millions of different cells that make up its body.

Within each cell is a nucleus containing threads of a substance called "chromatin," which is the most wonderful of all living matter, for it controls all life. The picture in the previous page shows how chromatin threads form tiny rods, which split in halves and divide into two equal groups, and how each of these groups becomes the nucleus of a new cell. The cells of an acorn multiply into a giant oak in just this way, and when you use up muscle cells in work or in play new cells to take their place are produced in the same manner.

But more wonderful still is the process of reproducing a new life. Consider a flowering plant, for instance. Down in the flowers, sheltered from harm, are many tiny delicate egg cells—the mother cells. A gust of wind, or an insect roving in search of nectar, brings to one of these a pollen grain from another flower. This pollen grain is the father cell. Left alone by themselves the mother cell and the father cell would die. But now the chromatin in the tiny father cell, following a mysterious instinct which lies at the very heart of life's secret, grows down into the flower and unites with the chromatin of the mother egg cell, and fertilizes it. At that moment the life of a new plant begins. The fertilized cell divides again and again, as described above, until it forms the tiny embryo plant, which lies folded up within the seed and is ready to unfold and grow when the seed germinates.

The process is similar among animals—a single tiny male cell penetrates and fertilizes a female cell, causing it to develop into a new animal. The chromatin in that first fertilized cell is derived from both male and female cells. That is why the new life resembles in part both parents.

Can you think of anything more wonderful than this strange power, locked up in a cell so small that the eye can't see it—the power to multiply and create bone and muscle, nerves and brain, the power to create new life, and to carry over to that new life those complex details of face, features, complexion, and even of mind and character which the parents possessed ?

web of life is so intricate as to baffle completely the imagination.

In the sea all is different. While there is often much plant life in the form of seaweeds (flowerless plants), especially along rocky shores, the wealth of plant life of the open sea consists of the invisible microscopic forms, especially the diatoms. About the animals of the sea there is always a peculiar fascination due to their abundance, their variety, and their strangeness. They are everywhere. Even the colder seas are populated by immense numbers of marine animals in great variety. Often along the shore there is a wealth of animal life the world over. The open sea has many peculiar forms at the surface, and still more peculiar ones at the bottom, even down as far as five miles. Fishes that are half mouth ;

FISH WITH HEADLIGHTS

Down in the dark ocean depths live numerous luminous fish, one class of which, Photoblephron, you see at the top of this page. These fish display a form of phosphorescence, shining night and day, which enables them to find their prey.

almost all of the sharks ; and other branches which might be named. Most of the life of the sea is fed, ultimately, by the microscopic plants that grow at the surface. Upon these tiny plants feed microscopic animals and small crustacea, even some fishes ; these in turn feed the larger animals, including fishes like the cod and sharks, and the whales and their relatives.

Among the most interesting and important of the biological interrelations of organisms is that of *parasitism*. There is scarcely a common form of life but has its many parasites. We think usually of the worms of many kinds that infest the intestine of man and most backboned animals ; and of the insects, and other parasitic forms in or on the bodies of most visible forms of plants and animals. But the most deadly parasites for man and many other animals are certain species of microscopic *bacteria* belonging to the plant world, and of *protozoa*, belonging to the animals. It is they that kill most of mankind and other animals. Bacteria cause some of the rot and blight diseases of plants, and their cousins, the *fungi*, cause the rusts and smuts of grains. Not all bacteria and fungi are bad ; many are useful in getting

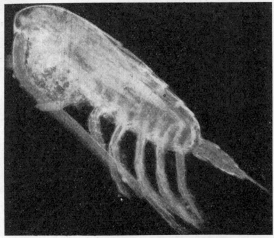

crabs and their relatives that are mostly legs and feelers ; starfish and their numerous relations ; even delicate jellyfishes and polyps are there. And think of the conditions at these great depths—the tremendous pressure of five miles of water ; the icy cold, even in tropical seas ; the absolute darkness, except that a good many forms are phosphorescent—for not a ray of light penetrates much beyond a few hundred feet ; the absolute quiet—for waves penetrate but a few feet.

All of the food and energy for this animal life at the bottom of the sea is from or near the surface, and consists of the microscopic forms of plants, or the small animals that have fed upon them. Over perhaps a hundred million square miles of the sea bottom is a deep " ooze," consisting of the skeletons of microscopic animals and plants that have rained down through the ages from the surface.

Many forms of life are peculiar to the sea. Whole branches of the animal kingdom are found here only and have never found their way into fresh water. Such are all the various forms of starfishes and their relatives ; almost all of the great branch which includes the jellyfishes and polyps ;

MARINE ANIMALS THE EYE CANNOT SEE

Here are two classes of microscopic sea animals, whose functions vary widely. The upper one is Calanus finmarchicus, the shrimp-like creature that forms the chief food of mighty whales ; while the lower photo shows Radiolarians whose shells help to form the rocks of the sea. Both animals are invisible to the naked eye.
Photos, F. M. Duncan ; E. A. Botting

rid of the dead bodies of larger animals and plants that would be in the way if not removed. (*See* Bacteria ; Parasites.)

Two or three branches of biology deserve special mention. One of the most fascinating and mystifying is the study of the reproduction and development of animals and plants—their embryology. The coming into being of an organism, especially one of the higher animals, remains one of the unsolved mysteries. Of course it is popular knowledge that the common forms of life arise from fertilized egg-cells, but it may not be so well known that this is just as true for an earthworm or an oak tree as it is for a man or a chicken. It is true for the whole living world that " like begets like " —that all plants and animals, simple as well as complex, arise only from parents like themselves. The simplest forms of animal and plant life consist of a single cell ; and they multiply merely by the single cell cutting itself in two, as described under Amoeba. It seems hard to realize, however, that a human being, with its infinity of characters, can arise from a tiny egg only a hundredth of an inch in diameter. It seems wonderful, too, that of three eggs, so nearly alike in size and appearance that it is difficult to tell them apart, one may give rise to a starfish, one to an earthworm, and the third to a human being. In reality these three eggs are very different from one another.

The origins of the higher forms of life seem so natural to us now that it is hard to realize that people formerly believed that even complex animals, such as earthworms and frogs, arose by " spontaneous generation," that is from non-living matter, without parents. It is only in recent years, however, that science has proved that the origin of life is the same for the simplest forms as for the highest—for the infinitely small germs of tuberculosis or cholera, and the whole multitude of plant and animal germs that have heretofore killed large numbers of mankind, as for mankind itself. Man can perform wonders in modifying the common forms of plant and animal life, but he can never create it.

Genetics, a new branch of biology dealing with the laws of heredity, dates back only to the beginning of the century. Since then it has been much studied, for there are " fashions " in science as well as in most human affairs.

It is common knowledge that plants and animals inherit the minutest characters from their parents. The amazing thing is that all the infinity of these characters. large and small, are carried by an unbelievably small amount of matter in the fertilized egg. Science tells us that all the people in the world at any one time have had their heredity carried by a total of less than ounce of matter ! Think of the wonder of the development of a human being, with his infinite characteristics—his features, colour of his hair and eyes, temperament, traits of character, and ability ! Or of a great redwood tree, that is to live for several thousand years !

Many plants and animals with hard parts have left remains in the rocks of the earth's crust which are called " fossils." The study of

PARASITE FLOURISHING ON ITS PREY *S. V. Waters*
Who would think this innocent-looking plant could have killed the great tree on whose stump you see it flourishing ? It is the deadly honey agaric fungus, and it will attack and kill fresh trees by sending out underground threads like bootlaces, and so transferring its hold upon them.

such remains is a branch of biology called *palaeontology*, although this study is oftener connected with geology, the science of rocks. Palaeontology more than any other science shows us the history of life in the world, through all of the millions of years of the infinite past. One of its most interesting revelations is that there are many forms of life that developed and flourished for ages, and then entirely disappeared from the earth. These include giant reptiles more than 50 feet long ; grotesque monstrous mammals ; giant mosses the size of trees ; and a thousand other interesting things are shown by the study of fossils. Large parts of some rocks are formed by these remains of plants and animals. The great deposits of chalk, for example, often thousands of feet thick, consist almost wholly of the skeletons of microscopic animals.

Several phases of biology may best be referred to by a brief history of the science during recent times. Great improvements in the microscope, as well as other improvements, along with the growth of science in general, made possible enormous advances during the 19th century.

(1) One of the first of these great advances was the realization that all plants and animals are made up of cells—that the cell is the unit of structure in all living things. In the simplest forms of life, both animal and plant, the whole organism is but a single cell. In all higher forms of life, Man for instance, the body is composed of millions and millions of cells, of many kinds, each kind specialized for some special use—muscle cells for motion, gland cells for secretion, etc.

(2) Following shortly upon the statement of the cell theory was the recognition that the essential part of a cell is its jelly-like substance, the protoplasm, mentioned above, and that this material is much the same in all living things, although differing infinitely in details in different types of animals and plants, and in different parts of the same complex organism. (See Biochemistry). When the egg develops into the human body, the protoplasm gradually becomes different in the various types of cells.

(3) The greatest advance in biology followed Charles Darwin's statement of the doctrine of organic evolution and the publication of his "Origin of Species" in 1859. The rapid acceptance of the view that living things are changeable, and that the diversified forms of life—of both animals and plants—have arisen by gradual changes from simpler forms, has had a very profound influence upon all fields of biological study. (See Evolution).

(4) Physiology is the study of properties, activities and functions in living things. Formerly it was limited almost wholly to Man, and was mainly a part of medical study. With the general growth of biology, physiology has been extended to the study of all living things. This has brought great benefit to medical science itself, for a large part of what is now known of human physiology was first worked out from studying frogs, cats, dogs, rabbits, etc. Fuller knowledge of plant physiology also has been of great benefit to agricultural science.

(5) Between 1865 and 1890 came many revolutionary discoveries by Pasteur and other workers, showing that fermentations and putrefactions are always caused only by minute organisms, and that these are always introduced from the outside, and never arise spontaneously. It was soon realized that most of the diseases of mankind and other animals are caused by these infinitely small bacteria.

(6) Ecology, the newest branch of biology, is the study of organisms in their relationships with their surroundings and one another. (See Ecology).

The least spectacular side of biology, but one

that is of fundamental importance, is the problem of arranging the various kinds of plants and animals in some orderly fashion. Modern classification of living things is called the science of taxonomy (from the Greek *taxis*, arrangement, and *nomos*, law). The aim of taxonomy is to catalogue all forms of life and to arrange them in natural groups, showing the relationships that exist between them.

According to the present system of classification, living things are separated into two *kingdoms*, the plant kingdom and the animal kingdom. Each of these is subdivided into

Geological Museum
ANCIENT LIFE SO LIKE TODAY'S
This prehistoric fern, found in a coal seam in Somersetshire, tells us something of the vegetation that covered England long before the great Ice Age. The study of fossils (paleontology) is a most fascinating pursuit, for it enables us to see that the living forms of millions of years ago were linked to those which flourish at the present time.

phyla, which place together the organisms that seem to be constructed on the same general plan. Each phylum is arranged into *classes* composed of organisms which, though similar to each other in their plan of structure, differ in some constant feature. Each class, in turn, consists of *orders*. Closely related groups in the orders are termed *families*. Each family is composed of *genera*, within which are still smaller groups or *species*.

Exactly what constitutes a species is a matter of debate; but in a general way, a species is a group of individuals essentially similar to one another in structure and capable of interbreeding. The scientific name of a species is always a binomial, that is, it consists of two words, as *Rana catesbiana,* the bullfrog, or *Quercus pedunculata,* the pedunculate oak. The first name shows the genus to which the species belongs. Sometimes slight differences, such as coloration or size, are used to separate species into still lower groups known as varieties ; these are designated by adding a third name. Thus, *Papilio glaucus* (var.) *turnus* is a dark form of the great yellow-and-black-striped swallowtail butterfly.

In some cases, finer divisions are made of a complicated group ; orders are split

Thos. Fall

BOTH DOGS, BUT HOW DIFFERENT!

The streamlined racing greyhound of England is seen top right, while below is the aristocratic Pekingese, unknown outside China until 1900. Despite the great and obvious differences between these animals, they are only breeding variations of the same genus, Canis.

up into sub-orders, families into sub-families, etc. Family names of animals usually end in *idae,* of plants in *aceae,* as *Canidae,* the dog family ; *Rosaceae,* the rose family.

How this system works out in practice can be seen from the following example. The common frog is classified as follows :

Kingdom, *Animalia* : all animals.
  Phylum, *Chordata* : vertebrates and their kin.
    Sub-phylum, *Vertebrata* : vertebrates only.
      Class, *Amphibia* : frogs, toads, salamanders.
        Order, *Anura* : tailless amphibians.
          Sub-order, *Firmisternia* : frogs only.
            Family, *Ranidae* : true frogs.
              Genus, *Rana* : certain kind of true frogs.
                Species, *Rana temporaria* : the common frog.

Many scientists have contributed to the scheme of plant and animal classification, but the work of Linnaeus is noteworthy above all others. (*See* Linné, Carl von.) Linnaeus brought order to botany and zoology by arranging

organisms into genera and species. He introduced the principle of binomial nomenclature which has been universally adopted. By international agreement, the scientific name of a plant or animal must be the first specific name applied to it, and this should be uniformly used throughout the world. To avoid international confusion, the names are derived from Greek and Latin, or from proper nouns which are given a Latinized form.

Finally, it should always be remembered that biology, like any other science or field of human knowledge, grows by the labours and discoveries of thousands of men, whom an unthinking world often forgets. Partly these discoveries are made by men who have in mind their practical use in " applied science " ; partly they are made by men who work and advance science just for the sake of increasing man's knowledge of the world in which we live. Often the discoveries of the latter class in " pure science " prove to have revolutionary importance in their practical applications. Such were some of Pasteur's discoveries which helped to revolutionize medicine, and which made him, a biologist, perhaps the greatest benefactor of mankind in the 19th century. (*See also* Prehistoric Animals ; Botany, etc).

Birch. With its paper-white bark, slender spreading branches and delicate foliage, this tree, widely distributed through Europe, North America, and Asia, is both beautiful and graceful. There are several species of birches, most of them hardy and rapid of growth, though many of them are short-lived. The wood is close-grained, often with a beautiful " figure," and is used for making furniture and for ornamental and other purposes ; it also makes

BIRCH

excellent fuel. The bark is much more durable than the wood because it is proof against water, and long after the fallen trunks have rotted away, the encircling bark remains sound and intact. Baskets, boxes, and many useful and fancy articles are made from the bark, including the birch canoes of the American Indians, while large sheets of it are used for roofing in Scandinavia.

The silver birch (*Betula alba*) is well named, for if a beginner were to go into the woods to search for it he would know it at sight by its white or silvery bark. This white bark is marked with dark horizontal lines. It is always thin, for as the tree grows the older bark peels off in long papery strips, leaving the fresh young bark that has formed underneath it.

There are, however, two kinds of birch in England, the species *alba* being divided into the common birch, *B. pubescens*, and the true silver birch, *B. verrucosa*. The bark of the latter usually becomes dark and rugged for three or four feet from the ground. This does not happen in the common birch. In the silver birch the ends of the branches tend to hang down, so that it has a very beautiful drooping appearance. When these twigs are very long and feathery the tree is known as the weeping birch.

The leaves of the birch are small and roughly triangular in shape, with uneven saw-like edges and a sharp point. In autumn they become a beautiful golden yellow.

The buds of the male catkins may be seen in winter like twin fingers at the tips of the twigs. In spring these tumble out into beautiful long tails. About the same time the leaves begin to appear, and among them the female catkins. The latter are much smaller than the males, and at first stand upright, but later they thicken and hang down, and in autumn they remain after the leaves have fallen. But as they are shaken by the winter winds they gradually shed their tiny winged seeds.

H. Bastin

SILVER BIRCH—THE DAINTY BEAUTY OF THE WOODLANDS

Though small in girth, the white or silver birch (Betula alba) grows to a height of fifty feet ; its drooping masses of continually fluttering foliage, which never entirely hides the branches, make a lovely cloak for its slender form. On the left above, the sharply-toothed, wedge-shaped leaves are seen ; they are arranged spirally on the stem. Beneath, are the birch's male flowers, which are always in pairs and hang downwards, while the female at first stand upright like spikes.

Our CHARMING FRIENDS *in* FEATHERS

*T*he story of the birds—of their lives and loves, of their homes and their
evolution in the course of ages from the reptiles—makes fascinating reading.
Surprising, too, for most of us know all too little of the winged creation.

Birds. All creatures which bear feathers are birds, and for this reason they are the most easily defined. Feathers are out-growths

from the skin, like the scales of reptiles or the hairs of mammals, but they are much more beautiful adaptations to the life which birds lead. (*See* Feathers.)

Birds, with the fishes, reptiles, amphibians, and mammals, make up the division of the animal kingdom known as Vertebrates or back-boned animals. Because of the modifications necessary for flight, however, the backbone of a bird, like the rest of its skeleton, seems very different from those of the other vertebrates. If you examine the skeleton of a bird and compare it with that of a reptile or a mammal, you are impressed by the way in which Nature adjusts structures to suit different needs. Birds are believed to have evolved, during geological times, from a reptile-like ancestor; and the differences in their structure which seem so great today have been brought about by the birds learning to fly. Birds today do not have teeth, but many fossil birds had teeth.

The framework of an aeroplane or any flying machine must be very strong and compact, and at the same time very light. A bird is a flying machine, and its skeleton is its framework; and the more we examine it the more impressed we become with the wonderful way in which Nature has transformed each part to adapt it to the bird's needs. The backbone, for example, has been shortened, and the separate vertebrae of the trunk have been

fused with one another and with the pelvis to give it greater strength. The ribs are firmly attached to this and also to the breastbone, and they have overlapping appendages to give the trunk great solidity. All of the bones are hollow, to give them the least weight for their strength.

In an aeroplane the engine and the passengers and all the heavy parts are placed as near the centre of gravity as possible, and with a bird it is the same. The outlying parts, such as the head and tail, wings and legs, are made extremely light, and the heavy muscles that work them are attached to the trunk, only the tendons extending to the outermost parts. When one examines the skull one is immediately impressed with the thinness of the bones. There are no teeth, and the jaws, therefore, need not be heavy, for the work of chewing, which would require muscles and weighty bones, is performed by the gizzard, which is a modified portion of the stomach.

When we examine the tail, we see that the numerous vertebrae which make up the tail of a reptile are all shortened and fused into one little bone called the *pygostyle*. One is quick to notice that the largest muscles of the legs are located about the thigh bones, which are held close against the trunk and thus near the centre of gravity. As if to make up for the shortening of the leg which this position causes, the ankle and foot bones are fused and drawn out into a long slender bone called the *tarsus*, which is the only part of the leg that is usually not covered with feathers, and to which the toes are attached.

When we examine a bird's wing, which is nothing more than the bird's arm or front leg modified for the particular purpose of flight, we see how few heavy muscles are borne upon it. The strong muscles that manipulate the wings are attached to the keel of the breastbone, and are thus brought

BIRDS OF VERY EARLY DESIGN

The flight of birds was slowly developed, and here we see a pteranodon, a prehistoric bird, "taking off." It could not fold its wings properly, and therefore could not land anywhere but on a cliff, or some spot from which a shuffle and a flap would suffice to launch it again into the air.

From material supplied by Prof. D. M. S. Watson

close to the centre of gravity. The unnecessary bones of the wrist and hand are fused, only one finger remaining well developed. Thus in every part of the bird's anatomy, the original reptilian parts have been so transformed as to make the bird a perfect flying machine.

Another great difference between birds and reptiles is that birds, in common with the mammals, are warm-blooded animals. The chief difference between warm-blooded and cold-blooded animals is that the warm-blooded have a constant temperature, while the temperature of the cold-blooded animals varies with that of their environment. It is for this reason that reptiles become very sluggish in cold weather, a characteristic that would not fit in well with the needs of a flying bird.

We may assume, therefore, that one of the most important changes that took place in the development from the reptile was the change from a cold-blooded to a warm-blooded condition. This change brought with it many accompanying changes in the life of the bird, for it ordained that the bird's eggs, also, should be maintained at a constant temperature, and that the temperature of the young should not fall below normal. This resulted in the need for " incubation " of the eggs, the building of nests, and the care of the young, which take up so much of the bird's life today.

This is likewise one of the reasons for the comings and goings or the " migration " of birds, which makes their study so fascinating ; for if they were still cold-blooded animals they would undoubtedly " hibernate " during cold weather. It is also the reason for their enormous appetites. It is because Mother Nature developed in them a bodily temperature much higher than that of Man that their life processes go on at a much more rapid rate, causing their ceaseless search for food.

The eyes of birds are very highly developed, so that they can see great distances and follow rapidly moving objects. Thus a swallow or a night-jar dashing through the air at breathless speed is able to keep its eyes on a tiny insect which is also moving rapidly. The eagle or vulture, soaring almost out of sight in the air, has a special " third eyelid " with which it can cover its eye when flying into the strong sun, and yet still see. And these and other birds of prey will dart with the speed of a bullet to a tiny object a human eye would hardly notice at a distance of a hundred feet. Likewise birds can adjust their eyes for different distances quicker than can other animals, and in general their powers of vision are far greater than ours.

Berlin Museum

BIRD WITH TEETH AND FINGERS

Scientists can trace in many ways the relationship of birds to reptiles, and their theories are borne out by such fossil remains as these, which were found buried deep in rock in Bavaria. Study of the remains shows that " archaeopteryx " (ancient wing) had teeth as well as a beak, and both fingers and feathers on its wings. In other words, it was half a lizard.

This ceaseless search for food gives birds their great economic value, in keeping down the hoards of insects all over the earth's surface. " Without the birds, not only would successful agriculture be impossible, but the destruction of the greater part of the vegetation would follow." We can appreciate the meaning of this statement by a famous naturalist if we stop to consider the great reproductive capacity of most insects, particularly those that feed upon vegetation and are therefore dangerous to crops.

The common potato beetle, if left undisturbed, is capable of producing 60 million offspring in a single season—not, of course, all its direct children, but some of them its grand-, even great-grand-children, since there are several generations a year under favourable conditions. A common plant louse, which brings forth living young, has such a short life cycle that there may be 13 generations in a single season ; and inasmuch as each female brings forth at least 50 young, the number in the 13th generation alone would be 10 sextillion. If left undisturbed and given plenty of food, it would take any insect only a few years completely to cover the earth with its offspring. The need for birds and other enemies of insects is, therefore, very apparent.

The astonishing number of insects consumed by birds has been revealed by scientists in several ways—first, by watching individual birds in the field through powerful glasses and counting the insects eaten ; secondly, by examining the contents of crops and stomachs of birds that have been shot while feeding ; and third, by watching the life of the birds at their nests and observing the food brought to the young.

An American bird called the scarlet tanager was watched feeding in a tree infested with gipsy moths, and in 18 minutes was seen to consume 630 caterpillars. A northern yellow-throat, another American species, was watched feeding in a birch tree infested with plant lice, and in 40 minutes is said to have picked off several thousand of the little insects.

A pair of great tits was once watched while they were feeding their family on the caterpillars of the winter moth, which do an immense amount of damage to apple trees. In one hour the pair visited the apple trees forty-seven times and each time they carried back to their nest two or three caterpillars. From that it is easy to calculate the good the little birds do in a day, for when they are feeding their young they are kept busy from dawn to dusk.

A wren was seen to feed her young thirty-eight times in an hour, and the food she brought them consisted of aphids, which suck the juice of plants ; caterpillars, which eat the leaves ; and daddy-long-legs, the grubs of which destroy corn and grass by devouring the roots. Starlings, which feed largely on leather jackets (grubs of daddy-long-legs) and on wire-worms (grubs of click beetles) which also do immense damage to crops, bring food to their young about thirty times in every hour.

Even the common sparrow, which is a seed-eating bird and is detested by farmers because it devours their grain, is a real benefactor at nesting time. Seeds are not a suitable food for its young, so it brings them caterpillars instead, and in this way destroys hundreds of these pests in a day.

The most remarkable case of feeding on record is that of a wren, which fed its young 1,217 times in 15 hours and 45 minutes. It has been shown by experimenting with young birds that they require from one-half to their full weight of food every day in order to grow. Thus a young robin, when leaving the nest, requires several feet of earthworms each day to keep it satisfied.

It is not only by the destruction of insects that birds play an important part in the economy of Man. Many of them derive a large part of their food from the seeds of weeds, and so help in keeping down these pests also. Here again the amount which they consume is remarkable. From the crops of two seed-eating birds were taken 1,700 and 5,000 weed seeds respectively.

A third way in which birds help Man in his pursuit of agriculture is by eating the small rodents which are very destructive to grain and forage crops, and which frequently do much general damage in the farm or garden. The common meadow mouse is so prolific that in five years, if all the offspring of a single pair lived, they would number several millions. It is therefore necessary to have some natural check upon their numbers, and nature has provided the hawks and owls.

Each hawk or owl requires the equivalent of a good many mice a day in order to live, or several thousands a year. These birds, therefore, have a considerable money value to the farmer upon whose land they take up residence. It is a noteworthy fact that following the so-called " plagues of mice," when these pests overrun districts by the thousands, there is always a flight of owls, usually of the short-eared species. Nature thus regains her balance.

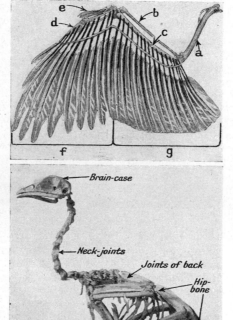

THE STRUCTURE OF BIRDS

The upper drawing shows the anatomy of the wing of a bird : a, humerus ; b, radius ; c, ulna ; d, hand ; e, bastard wing ; f, primary quills ; g, secondary quills. Below is the skeleton of a fowl showing the principal bones and joints. The figures indicate the toes.

A fourth way in which birds serve Man is as game. Certain birds, such as grouse, snipe, pheasants, woodcock, ducks and geese seem to serve Man best by providing him with food. None of them is particularly important as a destroyer of insects, and many of them become even harmful to agriculture if they occur in large numbers. Such birds are naturally prolific, and when properly protected by game laws are able to withstand, in suitable localities, the losses which they receive.

ROBIN REDBREAST AND JENNY WREN
Robins are amongst the most useful of our birds for they eat noxious insects of every type and the one above has a fat caterpillar in his beak. Right : a wren, one of the smallest of our birds, climbs back into her nest with a daddy-long-legs for her evening meal.
Photos, E. Hosking

Although practically all birds are valuable to Man in some one of the four ways mentioned, there are a few that usually prove troublesome at certain seasons of the year. Most birds, for example, are fond of small fruits, so that early strawberries, raspberries and cherries often suffer from their plundering. Where there is a plentiful supply of wild fruits, however, the cultivated fruits are left alone. Other birds, that customarily feed upon weed seed, often prove destructive in grain fields, so that it is necessary to frighten them away. Blank cartridges are as effective as the loaded ones, and they have the advantage of preserving the birds to feed upon the insect pests the following spring and summer. Crows, and some hawks, are enemies of the poulterer and the game breeder, but they serve a far more important function as destroyers of vermin, which would otherwise kill far more poultry than the birds ever do, and should therefore be spared.

When they are young rooks eat insects, but when they get older they turn their attentions to cornfields and young turnips. In winter, if the ground happens to be particularly hard, they attack the roots nearer the surface.

It is not merely because of their economic value, however, that birds are so extensively studied all over the world. Their cheerful songs, their bright colours, their many pleasing ways, serve to draw thousands of people from lives of confinement or inactivity into the woods and fields in the pursuit of recreation that is as health-giving as it is fascinating. Those who are unable to go far afield can, by suitably planting their grounds or offering food and water, attract dozens of these little feathered sprites close to their windows, where they can with little effort watch their many amusing and interesting ways and hear their cheerful songs. Though we may fix the money value upon the

W. A. Ramsay

A SCREECH-OWL WITH HIS DINNER
It is generally thought that all owls hoot, but the word hardly describes the ugly cry of the barn-owl or screech-owl. The screech-owl seen here carries his dinner—a vole—in his beak. The bird is the best known of all our owls.

insects devoured by the little hedge sparrow, we can never estimate the wealth which his cheerful song brings to those that have an appreciation of birds. And it is the small birds who are the singers generally, while the large ones sing little or not at all.

As soon as one begins to observe birds one discovers that the different kinds are found in different sorts of places. Some, like the robin and thrush, are widely distributed in woodlands, orchards, and gardens throughout the country, while others are restricted to certain localities or to particular environments. Thus

SCARING UNWELCOME BIRDS

Scarecrows are not always enough to keep the birds away from a field that has been newly sown, and though this queer figure may drive off the more timid ones, the boy with a clapper clears the field more effectively and quickly.

the nightingale nests only in the southern half of England, and the grouse is to be found only on the heather-clad moors. If one wishes to see moorhens and coots he goes to the ponds ; and if he wishes to see skylarks, meadow pipits, and lapwings, he goes to the upland fields. The study of *local distribution* offers many interesting problems to the amateur as well as to the scientific naturalist.

The study of the distribution of birds over the surface of the earth, or their *geographical distribution*, offers many other difficult and fascinating problems. If the world could be charted according to its families of birds rather than according to its races of people or its governments, it would make a strange map, because all the birds of the Northern Hemisphere are more closely related to one another than are the birds of adjacent islands of the East Indies.

Six main divisions or geographical regions have been recognized by naturalists when dealing with birds : New Zealand, Australian, Neotropical (South America), Indian, African, and Palaearctic (North America, Europe and Northern Asia). While a few birds are found all over the world, and others in two or more of these regions, the vast majority of species and many whole families are restricted to some one of these geographical regions. In travelling round the world, therefore, one would expect to find greater difference between the birds of North and South America or between those of Europe and Africa than between those of Europe and North America.

When we study the birds of the East Indian Islands, we discover some of the strangest facts of distribution, for some of the islands lie in the Australian region and some in the Indian, and the line between the two is very sharp. Thus the islands of Bali and Lombok (in the Malay Archipelago just east of Java), though but 20 miles apart, differ as greatly in their animal life as do Africa and South America, suggesting that the two islands had never been united and that the deep strait separating them marked the dividing line between the Australian continent and that of Asia—Bali belonging to Asia and Lombok to Australia.

In consideration of the geographical distribution of birds, the home of each species is considered to be that place where it builds its nest and raises its young, but many species migrate with the change of seasons from one region to another. Thus many of our nesting birds spend the winter in Africa.

In all the fields of nature study you will find nothing more wonderful than this seasonal migration of birds. The swallow that visits Britain in summer travels 5,000 miles over land and sea to his winter home in South Africa. The golden plover wings a 2,000-mile flight over the Atlantic from Labrador and Nova Scotia to South America without a stop ; while his relatives on the Pacific coast each year travel the 2,000 miles from Alaska to the Hawaiian Islands and back again. Not all birds, of course, migrate beyond our shores, for woodpeckers, nuthatches, tits, grouse, and a number of others are permanent residents of Britain. But swallows, swifts, ducks, warblers, flycatchers, thrushes, and many other species join the yearly migration. (*See* Migration).

During the winter the birds travel about in scattered groups searching for food, the sexes sometimes in different flocks, as, often, in the case of the chaffinch. With the approach of spring the birds begin to feel the instinct to move northward. Southern birds, of course, as for instance those migrating from southern to northern Australia in autumn, move south-

SOME FINE SPECIMENS OF BRITISH BIRDS' EGGS

There is a reason for the varying shapes and sizes of birds' eggs. For instance, Mr. Richard Kearton pointed out that birds which make round, cup-shaped nests, or incubate in holes, such as the Owl and the Kingfisher, lay eggs which are so shaped that they run no risk of rolling away and being smashed. The eggs of the Golden Plover, having their small ends all pointing to a common centre, practically form a square, so that, although the size of the eggs is abnormally large compared with that of the layer, the bird is enabled to cover them all at the same time. A key to this plate appears overleaf

Painted specially for this work by PERCY J. BILLINGHURST.

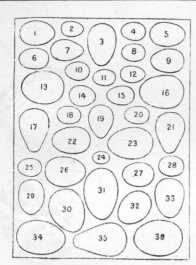

BIRDS' EGGS.—*Key to Colour Plate—*
1. *Magpie.* 2. *Robin.* 3. *Herring Gull.*
4. *Nightingale.* 5. *Jay.* 6. *Thrush.* 7.
Starling. 8. *Nuthatch.* 9. *Blackbird.*
10. *House Sparrow.* 11. *Swallow.* 12.
Hedge Sparrow, or Accentor. 13. *Kestrel.*
14. *Cuckoo.* 15. *Red-backed Shrike.* 16.
Sparrow Hawk. 17. *Ringed Plover.* 18.
Tree Pipit. 19. *Golden Plover.* 20. *Bull-*
finch. 21. *Dunlin.* 22. *Jackdaw.* 23.
Rook. 24. *Willow Wren.* 25. *Chaffinch.*
26. *Landrail, or Corncrake.* 27. *Quail.*
28. *Kingfisher.* 29. *Mallard.* 30. *Barn*
Owl. 31. *Great Northern Diver.* 32. *Heron.*
33. *Common Partridge.* 34. *Moor or Water*
Hen. 35. *Common Guillemot.* 36. *Red*
Grouse. The eggs are natural size with
the exception of Nos. 3, 19, 29, 31, 32, and
35. *which are half natural size.*

wards. The males are usually the first to start north, and arrive on the nesting grounds from a few days to a few weeks before the females. Once arrived, the males usually select the general locations where they wish to nest, and drive all rival males from these areas ; at the same time they try to entice the females to remain and to mate with them. As a rule, birds nest at the northernmost point of their migrations.

Even birds which do not migrate, and are therefore called residents, often move from one part of a country to another. Thus the curlew, which mates and spends the summer on the upland moors, commonly comes down to the shore to live in winter.

Often a male returns to the same spot year after year, and frequently his former mate returns also and they remate for another year. This may occur until the death of one bird, when the surviving member ordinarily finds a new mate and often returns to the same nesting site. Thus a pair of blue tits have been known to nest in the same jar for over 100 years, but undoubtedly they were not the same two birds. Although monogamy or a single mating for the year is the rule, a few birds, akin to our common poultry, such as the turkey,

LINING UP FOR A LONG FLIGHT

Such a scene as this may be seen anywhere in the south of England in the late autumn. The swallows are preparing for their winter migration to a more temperate clime, probably North Africa. They have lined up on telegraph wires and soon they will be off, not to return until spring comes to Britain again.

the grouse, the pheasant, and others, are regularly polygamous—that is, each male is mated to several females. Polygamy occasionally occurs among other birds, especially the wrens and blackbirds. Cuckoos do not have permanent mates, even for a single season, as they do not take care of their own young, but lay their eggs in other birds' nests. A bird of tropical America called the *Anis* is regularly communistic—that is, the members of this species build a common nest in which several females lay their eggs, and all help to care for the young.

Mating is never accomplished without a more or less elaborate courtship. It is during this period that birds are seen and heard to the best advantage, for the male birds try to make themselves as conspicuous as possible, both by their songs and by the display of their plumage. Of course all birds do not sing, and a few—such as the storks, the pelicans, and the frigate birds—seem to be voiceless in adult life. True song is confined to the

higher families of birds, and reaches its best development among the thrushes.

The vocal organs of a bird are somewhat different from those of a man, for instead of having vocal cords located in the *larynx* at the upper end of the *trachea* or windpipe, they have simple membranes which vibrate, located at the lower end of the trachea in a structure called the *syrinx*. The shape of this structure and the number of muscles which control the tension of the membranes vary with the different families of birds and produce the different songs.

Apart from songs we have other sounds. Thus the woodpeckers produce a loud tattoo by hammering with their bills upon a hollow branch. The ruffed grouse produces a loud drumming sound by beating the air with its wings ; and the snipe produces a " drumming " sound by mounting high in the air and diving so as to cause the two outer feathers of the tail to vibrate.

Even more interesting than the sounds produced by birds are the many curious displays

of plumage and courtship antics. The display of the peacock, the turkey, and the domestic fowl are familiar to all ; and many of the smaller birds can often be seen going through similar performances. Other birds, such as the pouter pigeons, the prairie chickens, and the bustards, have peculiar airsacs which they inflate during their courtship, giving them a very grotesque appearance. The skylarks perform feats of flying during their courtships that are quite spectacular. After mounting to such a height that they are barely visible, and after hovering and singing at that dizzy height, they suddenly close their wings and drop like stones toward the earth. One thinks they are about to dash themselves to pieces, when they gracefully spread their wings and alight.

Many of the albatrosses and cranes, and certain small birds as well, have elaborate series of hops, skips and bows which might be likened to old-fashioned dances. Among the most elaborate courtship performances are those of the bower birds of Australia, which build little bowers of twigs or plant stems. These bowers are entirely distinct from their nests, and are usually decorated with bright berries, shells, or flowers, which are renewed as soon as they wither. (*See* Bower Bird).

After mating, birds usually set about nest-building immediately. Although the male has already selected the nesting *area*, the female usually selects the exact nesting *site* and builds the nest, the male standing guard near by or accompanying her in her search for nesting material, and permitting no other male to approach within his territory. The character of the nest depends upon the species of bird and the family to which it belongs. It has

undoubtedly had its origin in the requirements of the young —how long they must use it and the dangers to which they are exposed—together with the intelligence of the bird in meeting these requirements.

When birds evolved from their reptilian ancestors, they naturally at first laid their eggs as do the turtles and lizards today, burying them in the sand or hiding them in holes in trees. But as they became warm-blooded creatures and the need for incubation arose to keep the eggs at a constant temperature, it was necessary to lay them above ground, so that they could be brought into contact

N. Kingston; D. Seth-Smith

COURTSHIP AMONG THE BIRDS
The males of such species as the peacock pheasant (top) and the turkey (bottom) carry out extraordinary manoeuvres in front of their intended mates, strutting and bowing, and displaying the beautiful marking of their wings to the best advantage.

with the bird's body. At first the birds probably did not even scratch depressions to keep the eggs from rolling about, but laid them on the flat ground as do the nightjars and guillemots today. The next stage was doubtless the scratching of depressions to keep the eggs from rolling, and we find this stage represented today by the nests of some of the plovers.

An advance from this stage was the addition of a lining to the depression, such as is seen in the nests of the lapwing. Such nests, however, give little protection against long spells of wet weather or against the numerous terrestrial enemies. It is easy to imagine that the birds that learned to raise their nests above ground, first on piles of vegetation and then into bushes and trees, were more successful in raising their young.

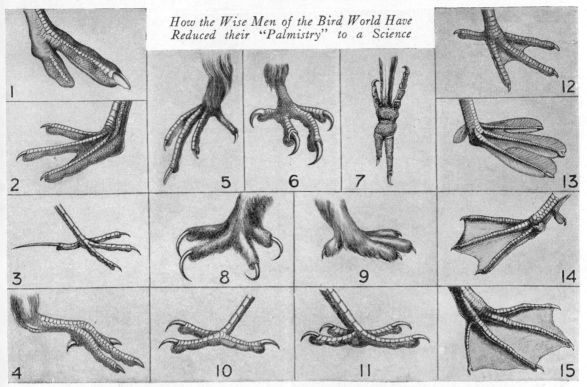

How the Wise Men of the Bird World Have Reduced their "Palmistry" to a Science

TELLING A BIRD'S FORTUNE BY ITS FEET

The study of feet among the birds may be called a scientific kind of " palmistry." Here is what a bird " palmist " would say to an Ostrich on looking at that foot of his (1) : " Your grandparents of some millions of years ago had five toes. The other three have disappeared because your family have put in so much time running. The third toe has grown very big, while the fourth toe, the only other one you have left, is dwindling. In the case of your descendants it will probably disappear altogether, just as happened with the horse." Another thing the " palmist " would say to all these birds whose feet we see before us is : " Pardon me—it doesn't sound like a nice thing to say to you—but your early ancestors were reptiles." He knows it by those scales, except in the case of the Tawny Owl (8) and the Ptarmigan (9), whose legs and toes are covered with feathers. All the other feet are scaled : Plover (2), Skylark (3), Apteryx (4), Night-jar (5), Sea Eagle (6), Toucan (7), Three-toed Woodpecker (10), Green Woodpecker (11), Stork (12), Grebe (13), Merganser (14), Pelican (15). Feet 12 to 15 are clearly those of birds that frequent the water. In the Stork (12) the web reaches only to the first joint. In the Grebe (13) the web is attached to each toe, but these toe webs do not join. This makes it convenient for walking as well as swimming. Although Plovers (2) are water birds, they wade along shallow shores and so, instead of webbed feet for swimming, have long toes to distribute their weight as they walk over the sand and mud. A Woodpecker's feet (10 and 11) are arranged to give them a good grip on tree trunks. Toucans (7) like the Green Woodpecker have two toes projecting forward and two backward, while the Owl (8) can turn his third toe either backward or forward, as he chooses.

It is not difficult to select from the nests built by birds today a series which shows the probable evolution of nest architecture, from the crudest to the most elaborate. Thus, the simplest platforms of sticks are built in the trees by some pigeons and the herons, while the crows and hawks build more substantial structures of sticks with deeper hollows to hold the eggs and usually with linings of softer materials. Continuing up the scale we find the coarse twigs discarded for finer and softer materials, until we come to such nests as those of the American goldfinch, which are made almost entirely of plant downs or other woolly substances.

The highest type of nest is that of the weaver bird, with its long overhanging tube entrance, but those of our longtailed tit, golden-crested wren, and reed warbler are very wonderful structures, though many of the simpler nests show curious specializations. The nest of the

humming-bird and that of the chaffinch, for example, are covered on the outside with lichens and bits of bark, so that they resemble the surface of the tree in whose branches they are built.

In selecting their nesting material, birds ordinarily take that which is nearest at hand, so long as it conforms to the type of the nest which that species builds. Thus field birds ordinarily use grasses and hair, woodland birds use leaves and rootlets, and marsh birds use sedges and reeds, while birds nesting in ready-made holes often use no lining.

Some kinds of birds are much more adaptable than others in suiting their nests and nesting places to changed conditions, and these are the ones that have been able to hold their own and even increase in numbers with the coming of civilization into this country. The nuthatch, tits, starlings, etc., that utilize neat boxes instead of holes in trees ; the martins

'HOME, SWEET HOME' IN THE FEATHERED WORLD

Birds have widely-differing ideas as to what makes a comfortable home, as may be seen from the selection of nests illustrated in this page. The nightjar (1) builds no nest and lays her eggs on the open ground. The ringed plover (2) has primitive ideas of architecture, and only scrapes a hole in sand or shingle. The linnet (3) makes an ordinary nest of twigs and grass lined with wool. The reed-warbler (4) makes what seems to us a rather unsafe home, for it is built around swaying reeds well above the ground. The golden-crested wren (5) slings its nest from the branch of a tree. The long-tailed tit (6) builds a domed nest of moss, covered with lichen and lined with feathers.

Photos, A. R. Thompson; F. Jefferson; S. Crook; I. M. Thomson and swallows, that have deserted the cliffs for human habitations ; and especially the familiar house sparrow, are examples of this power of adaptation.

The time used to build a nest depends upon how much time the bird has before its first egg is ready to be laid. With ordinary birds the time required is about a week ; but there have been many instances—when the first nest has been destroyed and the eggs are ready to be laid—of birds building their entire nests in a day. Occasionally birds that are permanent

J. T. Newman: A. H. Willford

READY FOR THE FIRST VENTURE

Above are a group of young blackbirds, on the great day when they must try their wings for the first time, poised fearfully on the edge of their nest. Below on the left, a newly-hatched sandpiper leaves its nest never to return.

residents, or that arrive early in the spring, begin their nests long before the eggs are mature, and spend several weeks in building a structure that could be completed in a few days if necessary. At times certain birds simply mend old nests left the year before.

The eggs of birds are among the most beautiful creations of all Nature. They vary in colour from those that are as white as snow to those that are almost black, but the majority have a delicate ground colour and are spotted or streaked with much darker colours.

Many theories have been advanced to account for the coloration of eggs. It is almost certain that the colour, as originally developed, was of some value to the eggs, probably in rendering them less conspicuous ; for eggs like those of the woodpeckers and kingfishers, that have always been laid in dark holes where the colour would

not be seen, are pure white. Eggs such as those of the plovers and terns, on the other hand, that are laid in exposed places with no protecting nest, are coloured like the soil or gravel and are very difficult to find. The majority of eggs, however, that are laid in nests, seem to be conspicuously marked rather than otherwise, for they are white or some light tint in ground colour. In such nests there is no need for protectively coloured eggs, because the bird ordinarily selects a site where the whole nest will not be readily seen.

Thus it has come about that, with the evolution of nests, the need for protectively coloured eggs has disappeared and the pigment has lost some of its quality, causing the many variegated but conspicuous eggs that we find today. Indeed, it might even be an advantage for nest-building birds to have conspicuous eggs ; for if there is an enemy living in the vicinity that will sooner or later discover the nest, it is to the bird's advantage to have it broken up as soon as possible so that it can go elsewhere and try again before the season is too far advanced. If the nest remains safe through the first few days when the conspicuous eggs are left exposed, it stands a good chance of remaining safe through the entire period.

Ordinarily, one egg is laid each day, until the normal number for the species is complete, but this number varies according to the dangers to which the eggs and young are exposed. Many sea birds that nest on very high cliffs lay but a single egg, while the majority of game birds and water fowl, that have numerous enemies, lay from 10 to 20. The usual number for most birds is from three to five in each brood, but the domestic fowl reared " intensively " has been known to lay as many as 314 eggs in a year.

The size of eggs is fixed for each species, and varies from that of the humming-bird, little bigger than a pea, to that of the ostrich, which is between five and six inches in diameter. Occasionally, with very old domestic fowls or at the close of the egg-laying

period, very small eggs are laid. Occasionally also two or even three eggs become enclosed in a single shell, forming the so-called " double-yolked eggs." In general the size of the eggs varies with the size of the bird, but birds whose young are hatched blind and helpless lay much smaller eggs than those whose young are able to run about when hatched.

With the laying of the last egg most birds begin to incubate, but a few, like the owls, begin to incubate with the laying of the first egg, causing the young to hatch on different days. The time required for eggs varies with the size of the egg, though for some reason a few small eggs require a longer time than some of the larger ones. Thus, while the eggs of the white-throat require but 12 days, and the eggs of the robin but 14, the eggs of the humming-bird require 15 days to hatch. Hens' eggs require 21 days, ducks' 27, and geese's 35. In addition to being maintained at a constant temperature by the heat of the bird's body, the eggs have to be regularly turned by the old bird, and occasionally moistened to keep the pores in the shell open and the membranes which line the shell moist so that the embryo can breathe.

With most birds the work of incubation is performed entirely by the female, the male either feeding her on the nest or standing guard by the nest while she flies off to feed. With some species, usually those in which the males are as dully coloured as the females, the males share the duties of incubation ; and in a very few the cock bird actually sits most of the time !

There are two types of young birds—those that remain helpless in the nest for some time, and those that can run about as soon as hatched. The first class are hatched blind and helpless, with only a scant covering of down. Their parents build well-formed nests in which they remain for varying lengths of time—from a week in such ground-nesting species as the skylark, to a year in such birds of flight as the condor and the wandering albatross. The young of the second class, on the other hand, like those of the domestic fowl, are fully covered with down when hatched, have their eyes open almost immediately, and are able to follow their parents about in their search for food. They remain in the nest only a few hours, and their parents must, therefore, be birds that live on the ground or in the water.

All young of the helpless type are fed at first on partially digested food brought up from the crop of the parent bird. Doves, petrels,

HUNGRY BIRDS MUST BE FED
The young of some birds are fed from their mother's gullet, and at the top we see a shag feeding in this fashion. The starling, however, is fed in the more usual way ; the bird seen on the left in the lower illustration is obviously enjoying the fine meal offered by its mother.
Photos, H. Mortimer Batten: W. F. Cassie

albatrosses, and a few other birds continue this method of feeding as long as the young require care ; but the majority of birds soon begin to bring fresh food to the young. This is usually carried in the bills or in the talons of the old birds ; but to this, as to all rules, there are again exceptions.

Most parent birds put the food into the open mouths of their young, and are careful to pop it well into the throat so that it cannot fail to go down. The young pigeon, however, thrusts its head into the open mouth of its parent and sucks a milky fluid which is secreted in the crop of the old bird. The young cormorant acts similarly, but instead of milk takes tit-bits from its mother's lucky-bag of half-digested fish.

The food of most young birds consists of insects at first, this being varied later by fruits or even seeds with some species. The insects are placed far down into the throats of the young birds, which normally stretch up their necks and open their mouths widely at the approach of their parents. Swallowing is entirely automatic, and unless food is placed beyond the base of the tongue, the muscles do not act and the food remains in the open mouth unswallowed. There is likewise a nervous adjustment to prevent the young from being overfed, for after each has received sufficient food, the throat muscles refuse to work, and the food remains unswallowed.

After feeding, the parent bird always inspects the mouths of the young, which usually remain wide open, and if any food remains unswallowed she removes it and gives it to one of the other young. As stated earlier in this article, the amount of food taken by young birds is surprising, for they require from one-half to their full weight of food each day in order to grow. To keep up this supply both parents work from early morning until nearly dark. In a few cases, like that of the humming-bird, the male bird never assists in the care of the young ; but in most cases the male is even more industrious than the female, and is often considerably more courageous than the mother bird in the presence of any danger that threatens. After each feeding the nest is scrupulously "spring-cleaned." Flesh-eating and fish-eating birds are exceptions to this rule.

Baby Birds' First Feathers

A few young birds of the helpless type, such as kingfishers and swifts, are absolutely naked when hatched, but the majority have a scant covering of down on the back and on the top of the head. Feather growth starts immediately and within a week or ten days the majority of small birds are fully covered with feathers, and within ten days or two weeks are able to fly. The largest birds of flight, however—the condor and the albatross—as already indicated, do not learn to fly for nearly a year.

The first covering of all young birds is called the *nestling plumage*. The covering of the fledgling is called the *juvenile plumage*, and it is worn only a short time after leaving the nest. It is then replaced by the *first winter plumage*. These feathers are worn throughout the winter, but in the case of most birds, towards spring they are replaced by the first breeding or *nuptial plumage*. This is replaced again in the autumn by the winter plumage.

The change from one plumage to another is called a *moult*, and takes place very gradually. When a bird is in good health only a few feathers are shed at a time, and these are replaced before others are shed, the whole process requiring from one to two months. The moult always begins at a definite place on the bird's body, and the feathers are lost in a regular order. Thus, in the wing, the first feather to be lost is always the innermost primary feather, and when the new feather replacing it is about half-grown, the next one is shed ; and so on, so that the bird is never deprived of the power of flight. In a few swimming and diving birds, such as the mallard or wild duck, that are not entirely dependent upon their wings for escape, all of the flight quills are shed at one time, and for a period the birds are unable to fly. It must be understood, however, that this is an exceptional form of moulting.

What Happens during Moulting

The summer moulting season usually begins in August and continues through a part of September. This is the most difficult season of the year to study birds, because during the moult they stop singing and seek seclusion, many species seeming to disappear altogether. During this moult every bird changes every feather on its body, and most birds that have been brightly coloured during the breeding season now assume sober colours, usually like those of the female. Thus the male linnet, which during the summer has a blood-red breast, appears with a buff breast like the female. During the spring moult, only such feathers are replaced by birds as are necessary to bring them into breeding colours. Thus the black-headed gull, which has a white head in winter, sheds only the feathers of its head.

Some birds appear to change their colours without moulting by a process called *feather wear*. This occurs only with such birds as have their new feathers edged with brown or grey ; for these edges, by their overlapping, conceal the underlying main colour of the feather. Thus the blackbird appears largely rusty brown in its winter plumage, but, as spring approaches and the brown edges wear off, it gradually becomes blacker and blacker until, by the time the breeding season has arrived, its feathers are shiny black. Often some prominent mark is concealed in this way during the winter, as for example the black throat patch of the male house-sparrow.

It is impossible to imagine a colour that could not be matched by the plumage of some bird, but in spite of this fact there are only four pigments or colour substances found in the feathers of most birds—black, brown, red, and yellow. In a small group of African birds called touracos, a green pigment also is present; but all other greens, and all blues and metallic colours, are due to the *structure* of the feathers rather than to pigments. It is usually the superficial layers of cells that are prismatic in shape and cause the refraction that gives the colour to the feather. To see the colour at its best, therefore, the observer has to be in good light with the sun at his back. It is for this reason that it is often difficult to identify the birds one sees under unfavourable light conditions.

E. J. Bedford

THE OWL IS NOT AMUSED

This young long-eared owl, ruffled with anger, is showing off its slowly-developing plumage. The white downy breast shows the primary stages, while the wing feathers are more advanced. A bird normally changes its plumage gradually by moulting.

Occasionally birds are seen whose feathers are deficient in pigment. There may be only a few white feathers in the plumage, or the entire bird may be spotted, or it may be entirely white. In the latter case it is said to be a pure *albino*. Such birds must not be confused with those in which the feathers are normally white, such as the gulls and certain northern birds in their winter plumage. A true albino has no colour and can be distinguished by the pink eyes and pale beak and legs. Albinism may occur in any species. In a few species the red pigment occasionally becomes overdeveloped and the birds appear much redder than the normal coloration, irrespective of age or sex. This is well shown in the red and grey phases of the American screech owl and in certain other dull-coloured species, but it is a phenomenon of a different type from albinism.

When there is a difference in the coloration of the male and the female bird, it is usually the male that is brighter. Among British birds, the *phalaropes* (a group similar to the sandpipers) are exceptions to this rule, the females being brighter than the males. It is interesting to note in this case that the males incubate the eggs and care for the young, while the females go off by themselves; for it is believed that the dull coloration of most females is due to the need for being inconspicuous on the nest.

When the males and females are coloured differently in the breeding season, the male in its winter plumage usually takes on a coat very similar to the female. It is for this reason that so few brilliantly coloured birds are seen during the autumn migration and during the winters spent in the south.

When the male and female differ in colour, the young birds in juvenile plumage usually resemble the female. If both sexes are alike, the young are similar, unless the adults differ in coloration materially from the other members of the family. In such cases the young often show the characteristics of the family.

When one begins the study of birds one very soon realizes that some birds are much more easily seen than others; for certain birds, such as the tits and finches, are quite conspicuously marked, while others, for example the sparrows and shore-birds, are protectively coloured. The conspicuously marked birds are ordinarily shy birds and do not permit of very close approach, while those that are protectively coloured are quite the reverse. Moreover, plumage that seems conspicuous when we see the bird close up, or in unfamiliar surroundings, may be really protective in its favourite haunts.

This form of "camouflage" among birds is an interesting example of the manner in which Nature safeguards animals from their foes. (*See* Protective Coloration).

There are today between 13,000 and 14,000 species of birds found in the world. Before anyone can handle conveniently any such large group of objects or facts it is necessary that they be systematically arranged, and this arrangement is called classification. In the classification of birds similar animals are put together in groups and similar groups together in larger groups, etc., their classification being based upon their *structure* rather than upon external similarity. Thus, all birds comprise the class *Aves* of the phylum *Vertebrata*. Below this, they are grouped into orders, with the termination *-formes*, as for instance *strigiformes*, the owl-like birds (*strix* is the Latin for an owl); and, finally, families, termination—*idae*.

BEAUTY IN THE WORLD OF WINGS

No wonder these two swans look proud, with their family of ten cygnets swimming along so daintily behind them! Although they are so very small, all the little ones are quite capable of looking after themselves in the water, as is indeed the case with most true water-birds that build close to their natural home. They are still wearing, as you can see, the first woolly down which covered them when they hatched only a day or two ago from the big nest of reeds and rushes—probably on the bank, or perhaps on an island in mid-water.

FEEDING TIME IN THE NIGHTINGALE'S NEST

Here is a mother nightingale at her nest, wondering what to do for those wide-open little beaks that are gaping up at her. She appears not to have any food for the youngsters, and perhaps that is why they are making such a fuss. There is something very reminiscent of the robin redbreast in the pose of the nightingale and the way in which its tail is held stiffly up, while the head is a bit on one side with a bright eye looking perkily at you ; and, as a matter of fact, the nightingale is just a big, brown cousin of the robin, with a wonderful voice.

'CAW-CAW' IN A TREE-TOP ROOKERY

We all know the rook, with its loud and cheerful " caw " and its broad blue-black wings, and here we can see one of these birds at home, just in the act of feeding its hungry family.   You can tell it's a rook, by the way, and not a carrion crow, because the base of its beak is covered with pale, bare skin ; if it was a crow, this part would be as black as the rest of the bird.   The rookery here is built high in the tops of beech trees, safe from most climbers and strongly built to withstand the swaying there must be when the wind gets up.

The business of feeding the young takes up all the time and energy of most birds, and hawks—like this cock sparrow-hawk—must have a very hard time when there are such hungry youngsters as this to find food for. You can see the remains of a bird on the edge of the nest, and one of the fledgelings is still picking at a last morsel. The sparrow-hawk, unlike the kestrel seen opposite, builds a large nest of its own—usually, as here, towards the top of a tall pine or other similar tree, where the thick foliage provides shelter and hides the nest from below

BREAKFAST FOR THREE IN THE KESTREL'S NEST

Three young kestrels, almost ready to fly, are here having what looks like their breakfast, for the clear light and the angle of the shadows show that it is an early-morning photograph. While one is receiving portions of a small bird from the parent bird, another is sitting looking out from the rotten tree-trunk, within which you can just see the third young hawk, bending over some more food. Down in the hollow, hidden from view, is the nest, probably the former home of some other bird, for the kestrel seldom makes a home of its own.

SONG-BIRD NEIGHBOURS IN THE HEDGEROW

Two of our commonest birds, the hedge sparrow (top) and the chaffinch (below), do a good deal to swell the clamou of bird song during the breeding season. The former bird—which is no sparrow and should really be called th accentor—has a quiet little warble in keeping with the subdued greys and browns of its plumage ; but the chaffinch one of the smartest of all our birds in his breeding dress, makes a loud, insistent and cheerful clatter which fairl rings out through the general noise. Both of the birds are here seen at their nests, feeding their ever-hungr families with delicious and appetizing insect titbits.

TWO GROUPS OF BIRDLAND'S NAUGHTY ROGUES

Few birds have such bad reputations as those you see here, the magpie (upper picture) and the jay (lower). The young " pies," as they are often called, will doubtless develop into a quartette of wicked rogues, for they are great egg-stealers and destroyers of young birds of all types. The jay, too, is partial to eggs, but, even more than that, it loves to gorge itself on ripening apples and pears. So the fruit-farmer as well as the gamekeeper shoots it when he can, and neither of them can be blamed for not stopping to admire the culprit's fine feathers. The magpie is a bird of the open, agricultural country, while the jay likes the shady woodlands.

A FINE PAIR OF HANDSOME WATER-BIRDS

Two of our most handsome birds are those you see here, one of them a member of the duck family, the other a typical wading bird. The sheldrake (top)—also known as sheld duck, burrow-duck, and by many other names—is a big bird, black and white and chestnut being his chief colours. The oyster-catcher, or " sea-pie " (below), is also a black-and-white bird, with brilliant scarlet legs and bill. He spends his time along the seashore feeding on molluscs—as his name implies—and, as you can see from the photograph, the nest is often actually surrounded with pieces of broken sea-shell.

Making Friends with the Birds

A WISE Doctor lives in a village in the West of England on the banks of a beautiful river, in the midst of a broad bird-haunted lawn and garden. He has the finest flowers, fruits, and vegetables in the town, although he never seems to take any more pains with them than his neighbours. People say he is lucky and has the "knack" of growing things, but the Doctor only smiles and says :

"I have all my little feathered friends to help me."

Few people understand just what he means by this, but it is simple, really.

As the years have gone by and the song birds —which are insect eaters—have become fewer, the Doctor's grounds are almost the only place in town where many of them nest. This is because he always has numbers of houses for them to build their nests in and rear their young, and also little shelves or "invitations to nest," as the Doctor calls them. These latter are placed under the eaves, in the tree-tops, and five or six feet high in the shrubbery, for birds that would not build in a house—such as the Thrushes, Flycatchers, Swallows, and Finches. Shelters are also put out where the birds can find refuge in advance of and during early and late storms, and they are always kept stocked with a special balanced grain mixture, suet and suet cake, so the birds know they can always find food and shelter in the Doctor's grounds. In winter, of course, strings of pea-nuts, coconuts cut in half, fat marrow bones and breadcrumbs are all put out for the hungry feathered folk. The Doctor's bird table, by the way, is at the top of a pole, overhanging so that cats and rats and mice are kept away. While the birds do not always patronize these shelters in the summer-time, they will fly for miles in times of stress to the Doctor's feeding stations, for food and shelter will always be there for them. Bird baths also are kept full of fresh cool water in the summer-time and warm water in the winter-time; and building material is put out in the branches of the trees and in the shrubbery. This consists of bundles of feathers or horsehair, and string or twine cut into six-inch lengths, or perhaps an old potato sack, cut in six-inch squares and tacked up in out-of-the-way places where it will not be unsightly, and yet where the birds' bright eyes can find it and ravel it out. Having attracted the birds to his garden and grounds, the Doctor keeps a sharp lookout for cats or other enemies.

Even among the birds themselves, of course, there are the inevitable bullies and thieves, not including the hawks which luckily do not visit the garden. But the Doctor knows whom to discourage and has little trouble.

In return for all these things, the birds act as policemen for the Doctor's garden. Let so much as a single caterpillar poke his nose through the hedge, and he is as good as dead ! And music ! Well, the Doctor has music free for the hearing throughout the whole summer day.

E. J. Hosking

ENJOYING THE HOME THEY NEVER BUILT

Those who live in the country may offer invitations to nest to many varieties of birds. But those who live in cities need not abandon the hope of seeing a nest built and young birds reared under their eyes, for common sparrows have often to do the best they can to find a place for their nests. A wooden nesting-box such as this will make a happy home for a sparrow family.

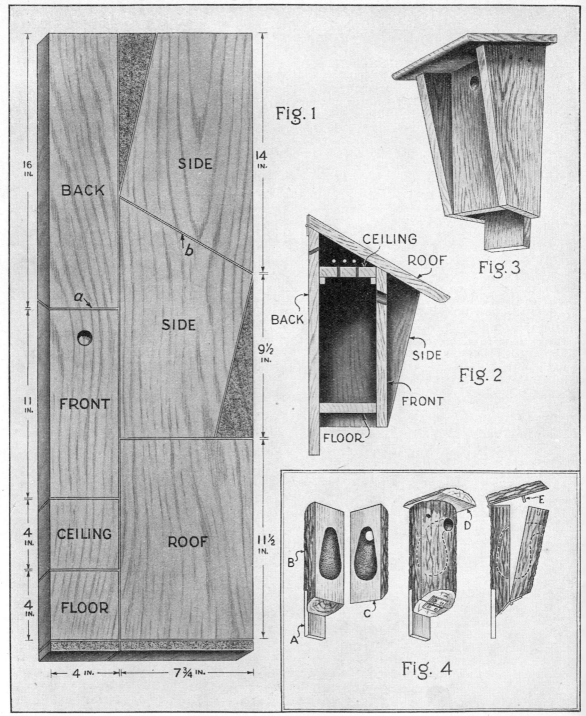

Fig. 1

16 IN.

14 IN.

BACK

SIDE

SIDE

↑ *b*

a

FRONT

11 IN.

9½ IN.

CEILING

ROOF

11½ IN.

FLOOR

4 IN.

7¾ IN.

Fig. 3

CEILING

ROOF

BACK

SIDE

Fig. 2

FRONT

FLOOR

B

A

C

D

E

Fig. 4

The first of these is designed for wrens. Notice in Fig. 1 that all the parts of this house can be cut out of a single 3-foot board of standard width and thickness (11¾ in. by ⅞ in.). The drawings make the design clear. The saw-cut marked *a* in Fig. 1 must be made at an angle of about 60 degrees. The two Sides are identical and the difference between the long edge (14 in.) and the short edge (9½ in.) will make the angle of the saw-cut marked *b* almost exactly 60 degrees. Figs. 2 and 3 show how the parts of the house are assembled. The distance between Ceiling and Floor should be about 8½ in. The Ceiling should not be nailed, but should rest on cleats so that, when the hinged Roof is raised,

the Ceiling can be removed for cleaning out the house. The entrance hole for the wrens must not be more than 1¼ in. diameter to prevent larger birds from trespassing. It should slope upward so rain will not run in. The ventilating holes around the top and through the Ceiling will help to keep the house cool in hot weather. Painting the house inside and out will make it last longer. Fig. 4 shows another type of house for wrens, tits, woodpeckers, etc. easily made by splitting and hollowing out a small log. The board A is used to fasten the house to a post or limb. B and C are hinged at the bottom; and the roof D holds the two together at the top by means of the short pin E

The dearest treat the Doctor can give to the boys and girls of his acquaintance is to invite a few of them at a time to a sunrise concert on his rose-covered side porch. There, as still as mice, they listen to the bird songs, look through the Doctor's big field-glasses, and watch the happy singers at work or play. There are Thrushes and Blackbirds, the chief songsters and the strongest; the cheery Wren and Robin Redbreast, the clattering Chaffinch and the Goldfinch with his sweet twitter; Warblers, too, sing from the quieter hedgeside at the far end of the garden and the Chiff-Chaff repeats his own name all day long.

The eaves of the Doctor's barn is a great place for Swallows, favourites of all the birds which actually nest on the house. A dozen or so of them skim and wheel about, the sun glistening on their iridescent blue-black wings and forked tails. They chatter, scold intruders, and sing sweet gossipy songs to each other. With them, too, are their cousins, the House Martins, smaller, with dark blue and white suits. The Wrens come right up to the house and sing from the roof, the low bushes, and the ground. Bill up, perky tail jerking about, the merry singer is a nervous little bird and scolds at times. "Five inches of brown fury in feathers," the Doctor called Mrs. Jenny Wren. She scolded everybody about the place, even Mr. Jay, who would have liked to steal her eggs!

On the house, too, against the creeper, lives the neat Spotted Flycatcher, which comes late in Spring but is soon hard at work eating the insects.

Ever so many more birds are to be seen in the Doctor's home grounds, as more than a hundred different kinds visit him every summer. Many of them also stay with him all the winter, such as the various Titmice, Nuthatch, Tree-creeper,

and Woodpecker. The Nuthatch is the little bird that gets the mud from the pond's edge, and sticks it all around the opening of its house; it knows the mud is there and can avoid it, while any other birds will find the door too narrow, if they try to enter. Most of the birds belong to the families of the Thrushes and Finches, the Woodpeckers, Flycatchers, and the little Warblers. You can tell what family a bird belongs to by its song and its food habits, as well as by its colours or its nest. How many of the Doctor's birds do you know?

One spring day each year the Doctor has a nest-building party. The boys bring houses of all shapes and sizes and empty boxes, ready to convert into houses and shelters.

"Years ago," the Doctor tells them, "when dead timber was not cut away nor old limbs trimmed from the trees, our feathered friends had no trouble in finding nesting places, but now this is all changed. So if we want to have birds for neighbours, we must put up houses and sheltered shelves in which they can build their nests and rear their young."

The Doctor has to be consulted very often, for even the openings of the boxes or houses must be made just the right size for the particular kind of bird the house is intended for. If the opening is made too large, the Doctor shows the boys how to make it smaller by placing a piece of wood over it with a smaller opening. Two sorts of these bird homes you can make for yourselves, if you follow the plans in page 530. One word of warning the Doctor always gives, and this concerns cats. "Cats take a terrible toll from our song birds," says the Doctor. "Every cat will catch at least 50 birds every year, so you must choose between the cats and the song birds. You can't have both." And so all the boxes must be cat-proof as well as water-proof.

E. J. Hosking

INSIDE THE SPARROWS' HOME

Sparrows build their nests anywhere where there is a solid foundation, but they have not the skill to construct such ingenious nests as some of those shown in page 516. Yet in a nesting-box like that in page 529 (an interior view is shown here) they will build a rough and ready nest, chiefly made of feathers, where they hatch out their young.

Birkbeck, GEORGE (1776–1841). One of the colleges that make up the great University of London is the Birkbeck College. George Birkbeck, after whom it is called, was the son of a banker, of Settle, Yorkshire. He was educated at Edinburgh, studying medicine, and for a few years he was a professor at Glasgow. In that city he started the Glasgow Mechanics' Institution, the first of its kind in the country.

Later, he began to practise medicine in London, and while there had a good deal to do with the foundation of the London Mechanics' Institution, which was opened in 1824. Of this institution he was the first president, and to it he lent £3,700 in order to build a lecture room. After a time the name was changed to Birkbeck Institution or College, and a home was found for it in Breams Buildings, Chancery Lane, London, E.C. Birkbeck was also one of the small group who founded University College, London. He died December 1, 1841.

Birkenhead. One of the most important seaports in the north of England is Birkenhead. It stands on the Cheshire or southern side of the estuary of the Mersey, opposite Liverpool, the two places being connected by the magnificent road tunnel opened by King George V in 1934, as well as by a railway tunnel. The town is quite modern and it was only in 1847 that the first dock was constructed, but after that its population grew rapidly and there are now 171 acres of docks. Many persons who work in Liverpool make their homes here, crossing the river either by the railway tunnel or on the ferry boats twice a day. There are a lighthouse and an observatory on Bidstone Hill overlooking the town, which has a population of about 150,000.

Birkenhead, FREDERICK EDWIN SMITH, FIRST EARL OF (1872–1930). Born in Birkenhead, young Smith won a scholarship to Wadham College, Oxford, and at the university he made a reputation as a scholar and a speaker. He became a lecturer and then a barrister, and in 1906 was elected M.P. for one of the divisions of Liverpool as a Unionist. He distinguished himself as the "rising hope" of his party, which was smarting under one of the greatest electoral defeats in its history, and in the years just before the outbreak of the World War was a leader of the Ulstermen in their fight against Asquith's Home Rule Bill. He was made a privy councillor in 1911 and in 1915, after he had been on active service in France, he was appointed solicitor-general. In a few months Mr. Lloyd George made him attorney-general, and in 1919 he became Lord Chancellor and was created a peer, taking the title Baron Birkenhead. He was one of the four British statesmen who signed the treaty with the representatives of Ireland in 1921. In 1921 he was made a viscount and in the following year an earl. In 1924 Birkenhead became secretary of state for India, but he retired in 1928 to enter business life. He died not long afterwards, on September 30, 1930. While he was Lord Chancellor he was responsible for drafting the Acts that altered the English law of real property, and some of his judgements in the House of Lords rank with the greatest of their kind.

Ambitious and adventurous, Birkenhead loved luxurious surroundings, and had a zest for the more robust forms of social activity. His amazing intellect and powerful physique made it possible for him to discharge his political and professional duties and yet have time for hunting, yachting and other diversions.

WHERE MERSEY TUNNEL ENDS IN BIRKENHEAD
Birkenhead is not beautiful, but this photograph from the air shows the docks, shipyards, factories and railway sidings which testify to its prosperity. Near the centre of the photograph can be seen the entrance to the road tunnel under the Mersey which connects the town with Liverpool on the opposite bank of the river. The tunnel is two miles long.

As "The Times" said: "The premature death that has quenched his vivid and always combative character has put the last enduring emphasis upon its vitality, and accentuates, as it were, the zest and recklessness with which Lord Birkenhead spent his venturesome life."

Birkenhead. BRITISH TROOPSHIP. The story of the wreck of the Birkenhead affords one of the most wonderful examples of discipline and bravery in the face of death that has ever been told. During the Kaffir War in South Africa, this paddle steamer was dispatched with nearly 700 troops on board as reinforcements to the British regiments on active service in Cape Colony. After a voyage of 48 days from Cork, the Birkenhead arrived at Simon's Bay on February 24, 1852. There it discharged a few troops, and the following night again put to sea in order to proceed to Algoa Bay.

Perhaps because the captain wished to make a quick passage, the vessel was kept too close to the shore, and within only seven hours from the time she left the harbour the Birkenhead struck a rock, at 2 o'clock in the morning. Immediately a great hole was torn in the bottom of the ship.

The bugles sounded, the officers instantly took command, and while the sailors were ordered to the pumps or their stations, all the soldiers were mustered on deck. Every officer and soldier stood steadily in rank.

Seven women and thirteen children were placed in a small boat, which was safely launched within twelve minutes from the time the vessel struck. What a heart-rending ordeal it must have been for these to pass silently into the boat, leaving loved husbands and fathers standing there so silently that even a word of farewell might not be said! No sooner had this boat been got away than the ship broke in two, and the stern half sank.

Still the men stood in rank awaiting the end, and the two senior officers who commanded

LAST MOMENTS ON THE BIRKENHEAD
The wreck of the Birkenhead on February 25, 1852, was the occasion of one of the greatest examples of discipline and self-sacrifice which the British Army has shown. Nearly 700 men stood steady and never broke rank so that the women and children should be saved while the troopship literally sank beneath their feet off the coast of Africa. This famous picture by Thomas M. Hemy gives a vivid representation of the scene just before the Birkenhead went down.

them told them not to jump overboard, as any attempt to get into the boat containing the women and children would certainly swamp it.

Soon after this the deck sank beneath the British soldiers and within twenty minutes of striking the rock the Birkenhead had foundered.

None of the women's and children's lives was lost, and altogether 184 persons were saved; but 454 officers and men were drowned.

Birmingham. This great manufacturing city lies in the centre of England, 105 miles north-west of London. The town was in existence before the Norman Conquest, and the manufactures of the city date at least from the early 16th century, as evidenced by Leland's

Birmingham claims to be one of the best-governed cities in the world, a reputation it began to win when Joseph Chamberlain was mayor, and to the same man it owes its university. This was founded in 1900, and has a fine range of buildings at Edgbaston, where all the requirements of a modern seat of learning are found. King Edward's grammar school, an old foundation, has been moved to a site away from the centre of the city. There are several technical schools, including one at Aston and another at Handsworth.

The Council House, begun in 1874, proved too small for the work of the city and a handsome extension, connected to the older building by a bridge, has been erected. Adjoining it is the Art Gallery, with a fine collection of pictures.

In 1904 Birmingham became the seat of a bishopric with St. Philip's Church as the cathedral. St. Martin's Church, in the Bull Ring, another fine building, is the parish church. There is a Roman Catholic Archbishop of Birmingham, whose cathedral is in Bath Street. Birmingham has a fine water supply drawn from

Itinerary (1538), in which he writes of Birmingham: "There be many smithes in the towne that use to make knives and all manner of cutlery tooles, and many loriners that make bittes (for horses), and a great many naylors (nail makers) so that a great part of the towne is maintained by smithes, who have their iron and sea-cole (ordinary coal) out of Staffordshire."

The leading industry today of the district of which Birmingham is the centre is metal-working of all sorts—founding, rolling, stamping, plating, drawing, etc.—and the products include machinery, engines, iron roofs, girders, and all kinds of industrial wares. The manufacture of railway carriages is an extensive industry, and Birmingham is a large centre for the manufacture of motor-cars, tyres, and other accessories.

Small arms, watches and clocks, electrical apparatus, brass work of all sorts, gold and silver articles and jewellery, screws and nails, and steel pens are manufactured in huge quantities, and buttons, hooks and eyes, pins, etc., are also produced. It is said that over 1,200 trades are carried on in the city. Near Birmingham the steam engine was perfected by James Watt and Matthew Boulton, and their famous Soho works are one of the most precious heritages of the city. Four miles away is Bournville, with its famous cocoa and chocolate works, set in a garden city.

Dixon-Scott

BIRMINGHAM: CAPITAL OF THE MIDLANDS

The great industrial city of Birmingham is reputed to be one of the best governed in the British Isles, and it is justly proud of its fine buildings and spacious streets. Above is the City Museum and Art Gallery, opened in 1885, which is housed in a wing of the Council House. Below is Corporation Street, one of Birmingham's chief business thoroughfares.

a great reservoir at Rhyader in Wales, about 80 miles away. It was completed in 1905.

The city extends over 79 square miles and includes Aston Manor, once a separate borough, and other outlying districts. It possesses many parks and open spaces, one being Aston Park, and land on the Lickey Hills in Worcestershire. It is governed by a lord mayor and a council and sends 12 members to Parliament. The population is over 1,000,000.

Until 1769 Birmingham was ruled chiefly by the lord of the manor through his two manorial courts. In the court baron by-laws for local government were made and local business was transacted ; in the court leet cases were tried, stewards appointed, bailiffs to superintend the markets were elected, and constables appointed. The affairs of the parish were looked after by the churchwardens and overseers and the surveyors of highways were chosen at parish meetings. There were two bailiffs. The high bailiff saw that order was kept and that no " unlawful games to the injury of ignorant persons and thoughtless youths " were played. The low bailiff summoned the juries.

Biscuits. Our word " biscuit " comes from the French, and means " twice cooked." This is because biscuits were once subjected to two bakings. They are really a form of bread made in the form of thin, flat, dry cakes. All biscuits are fermented except sea-biscuits, also known as ship bread, the ingredients of which are simply wheaten flour, water and common salt.

Of recent years biscuits of all kinds have become enormously popular. Elaborate machines mix the dough, roll it out into sheets, and stamp these into plain or fancy forms which hold together until after they are baked. There are also ingenious contrivances for icing them, and for doing the various things necessary to turn out the many appetizing kinds of biscuit now offered us by every grocer.

Bismarck, Otto von (1815–1898). In July, 1870, three men sat about a table in a hotel in Berlin, nervously awaiting a dispatch from their king, William I of Prussia, who was at Ems. The French ambassador had sought an interview with him there, and on its outcome might hang the issue of peace or war. Presently a servant entered bearing the looked-for message· He handed it to Bismarck, who read it to his two guests—Moltke, who was the chief of the Prussian army staff, and Roon, who occupied the office of minister of war.

In telling of the incident afterwards, Bismarck said : " As I read the dispatch to them, they were both actually terrified, and Moltke's whole being suddenly changed. He seemed to be quite old and infirm. It looked as if our most gracious majesty might knuckle under after all. I asked him (Moltke) if, as

things stood, we might hope to be victorious. On his replying in the affirmative, I said, ' Wait a minute,' and, seating myself at a small table, I boiled down those 200 words to about 20, but without otherwise altering or adding anything. It was the same telegram, yet something different—shorter, more determined, less dubious. Then I handed it over to them, and asked, ' Well, how does that do now ? ' ' Yes,' they said, ' it will do in that form ! ' "

The Ems telegram, thus altered, was interpreted in the press to mean that the king had been insulted and had snubbed the French envoy—which was not the case. In both Berlin and Paris the war spirit rose to fever heat, and on July 19, 1870, France declared war. Thus by trickery Bismarck became the real founder of the German Empire.

By birth and tradition Bismarck was a member of the conservative Prussian Junkers or landed aristocracy. He once said : " From the beginning of my career I have had but one guiding star : by what means and in what way can I bring Germany to unity ? " He early saw that Austria was the obstacle.

Bismarck recognized that Prussia must become a great military power if it would defeat Austria. So he set to work to secure a reorganization of the Prussian army. To accomplish this, for four years he was obliged to wage an unceasing conflict with the Prussian legislature, which refused to vote the necessary funds. His first chance to use his reorganized army

BISMARCK AND HIS FALLEN FOE

This famous picture by Wilhelm Camphausen shows Bismarck with Napoleon III on the morning of September 2, 1870, the day after the battle of Sedan. The " Iron Chancellor," as he was called, had succeeded in his scheme against France far beyond his expectations, for on the previous day the main French army had surrendered and Napoleon III, the Emperor of the French, who lost his throne as a result of his defeat, had been taken prisoner.

came in 1864. In that year a war was successfully waged by Austria and Prussia against Denmark for the possession of the two little provinces of Schleswig and Holstein. As a result of this war the two duchies came under the control of the victors. Then, in 1866, Bismarck picked a quarrel with Austria over the management of the spoils. Within the brief period of seven weeks Austria was defeated.

When Bismarck tricked France into declaring war, as described above, the South German states joined Prussia, and after one of the most humiliating wars in her history France saw the victorious German troops march through the streets of her capital. On January 18, 1871, Bismarck's goal was won with the proclamation of the new German Empire at Versailles.

For 20 years Bismarck continued to govern the country he had made. He built up its manufactures and its trade until Germany was the leading country on the Continent. But when the young William II came to the throne of Germany, he wished actually to rule instead of leaving affairs in the hands of Bismarck. So the old pilot was deposed from power.

Bismarck's full name was Otto Eduard Leopold, Prince von Bismarck-Schönhausen. He was made Count after the Danish War, and a prince after the war with France. After his resignation in 1890 he was created Duke of Lauenburg. The third volume of his memoirs, because of its damaging reflections on the Emperor William II, was suppressed until after the revolution which made Germany a republic. Bismarck's published volume of letters to his wife gives us pictures of that affectionate family life which is one of the best features of the German people.

Bison.

Commonly called "buffalo" in the country of its origin, the American bison (*Bison americanus*) is the largest and most celebrated of all American hoofed animals. Originally it was found on two-thirds of the continent of North America. Its range extended from Mexico to the region of the Great Slave Lake in Canada, and from Pennsylvania and the Carolinas to the Rocky Mountains.

'DROPPING THE PILOT'
This famous cartoon by Sir John Tenniel appeared in "Punch" just after the young Emperor William II, leaning over the ship's side, had dismissed Bismarck, represented as the pilot.
By permission of the proprietors of "Punch"

Its food was the herbage of the plain and prairie.

The number of bisons at the time America was discovered has been estimated at from 30,000,000 to 60,000,000. In 1870 the number of survivors was estimated at 5,500,000. The vast herds sometimes derailed trains in the west and stopped boats on the Yellowstone and Missouri rivers. Colonel Dodge reports that, while travelling in Arkansas in 1871, "for 25 miles he passed through a continuous herd of buffalo," and other evidence shows that this same herd was fifty miles across! The completion of the transcontinental railways and the introduction of the repeating rifle about this period soon almost completed their destruction.

To the Indians of the great plains, the bison was the most important game animal. The hides furnished him with the material for tepees and robes. He lived a good part of the time on the fresh meat, which is almost as good as beef; and for winter the northern tribes made a preparation of the dried meat with berries and fats, called "pemmican." This furnished a nutritious and well-balanced ration in small space.

In 1883 the famous Sioux chief, Sitting Bull, and his band of warriors are said to have slaughtered the last thousand head in southwestern Dakota, leaving less than 1,000 head then alive on the American continent, two-thirds of those being in Canada.

The bison's massive head is his most characteristic feature. His bow-shaped back, different from that of the ox, and the unusually long vertebral spines increase the size of his shoulders. The convex shape of the frontal bone makes the forehead bulge. Over all the bulk of bone and powerful muscles of the neck and shoulders is the great shaggy coat of curly brown fur. The hair on the head falls over the eyes in a thick mane. The forequarters are heavier and higher than the haunches.

The adult male stands $5\frac{1}{2}$ feet high at the shoulders, is 9 to 10 feet long, and weighs from 1,600 to 2,000 pounds. The female buffalo is smaller, for a large cow does not exceed 1,200 pounds in weight. The horns are short and

VANQUISHED MONARCHS OF THE PLAINS

Even the protected Bison herds of today go into stampedes. The thundering herd at the top is re-enacting for a moving-picture camera scenes of the early pioneer days, when Bisons, sole monarchs of the plains, roamed in countless thousands.

Only a few centuries ago the Aurochs, or European Bison, ruled the plains of Europe. Before the World War small herds still were scattered over the continent. Today only a few individuals of the original stock are left. The small herd below is reared on a farm in Hungary, but these animals are not pure blooded stock.

The American Bison disappeared from the plains only a few decades ago, but the Royal Bison has not roamed the earth since the Stone Age. We know of him from pictures drawn and carved by Cavemen artists who hunted him thousands of years ago, and from his fossil remains found on both the American and European continents. This copy is from a painting by Charles Knight in the American Museum of Natural History.

The train hold-up shown in the old engraving at the right took place in 1869. This was a common incident in the history of the first American railways. Often trains were blocked for hours by vast torrents of stampeding bisons. Engineers tried running through the masses, but their engines were easily hurled aside, and the stampede went on.

black, and in the males are thick at the base, tapering abruptly to a sharp point as they curve outward and upward. In the female they are more slender. The hoofs are short, broad and

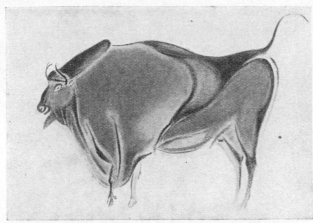

EUROPEAN BISON OF 20,000 YEARS AGO

In prehistoric times bisons wandered all over Europe, and fossil remains of them have been found even in the Thames valley. This drawing shows how a bison appeared to prehistoric Man, for it is one of the marvellous wall paintings in the Altamira cave at Santander, in Spain, which were made in the Stone Age.

black. The general colour is pale brown, darker on the head and shoulders and underneath. The hair on the forepart of the body is 10 to 15 inches long on the head, 6 to 8 inches long on the neck, shoulders and forelegs, and 10 to 12 inches under the chin, where it resembles a beard and is so called. The hinder and lower portions of the body are covered with short, soft, woolly hair. The tail ends in a tuft of coarse hair 12 to 18 inches long.

The long hair on the forepart of the body is permanent, but that on the hinder portions is shed annually, beginning in March. By early summer this part of the body is quite naked and very sensitive. In order to escape the attacks of flies and other insects, the bison seeks out muddy sloughs and shallow ponds, where it wallows until its body is covered with clay, which bakes in the sun and forms a protective armour, lasting for days.

The new coat is fine by October, and at its best in November and December. The hide is then valuable as fur. A half-century ago " buffalo coats "— overcoats made of the fur of young bison—were in common use and remarkably cheap. Such coats today would probably sell for £100; formerly, they sold at from £3 to £5. A prime " buffalo robe " could be exchanged for a pound of tobacco.

Under primitive conditions bison herds moved from one feeding ground to another, going northward in the spring and southward in the autumn. The southward migrations occurred in herds numbering millions of animals. They travelled hundreds of miles, swimming mighty rivers and climbing or descending steep banks, cliffs and precipices. They followed the same routes year after year, usually in single file, making paths that became lasting trails two or three feet deep. The northward movement began in the spring after the calves were strong enough to travel. In this movement they separated into smaller herds, the bulls occupying the outer circle and the cows and calves the inner. When danger threatened the herd closed in, the bulls facing outward to protect the weaker members.

The principal enemy of the bison, apart from the Indians, was the grey or buffalo wolf which hung in packs about the outer edge of the herds, and often succeeded in isolating and capturing a calf in spite of all vigilance. The grizzly bear was the only animal that could ever vanquish a buffalo bull in single fight.

It required heroic efforts to save the bison from complete extinction. It was not until 1902 that the U.S.A. Congress took the first

TYPICAL AMERICAN BISON OF TODAY

In America bisons were once so numerous that a single herd was estimated to consist of 4,000,000 animals, and to cover an area 50 miles by 25 miles. Now the few that remain are carefully guarded, and this one was photographed in the Buffalo National Park, where it need no longer fear the hunter.

steps towards preservation when it voted a sum of money for the purpose of assembling survivors in the Yellowstone National Park. As the bison breeds readily in captivity its numbers have steadily increased. The Canadian herds now contain over 13,000 head, chiefly in a vast park in Alberta; and there are, besides, many thousands of bison in the United States, the largest single herd being in the reservation on the Yellowstone. The " cottalo," part buffalo and part common cattle, has been bred in Canada.

The European bison was common in Europe two or three thousand years ago, and later in the Harz Mountains, but is now reduced to a few herds in the Zelentschek district of the Caucasus Mountains and in a few private preserves. The European bison is somewhat smaller than the American, and since it lived in forest country it ranged in smaller herds: it is sometimes called the *aurochs*, but this name is more properly reserved for the long extinct wild cattle of Northern Europe. It is stated on good authority that the males outlive the females by about ten years. If this is true of the American species, it explains why in every herd, as many observers have remarked, the bulls always outnumber the cows. No effort has been made to tame the bison.

By an unusual mischance the first skeleton of an American bison, exhibited in Paris in 1819, contained 15 pairs of ribs. As a result of this freak, which probably occurs only once in many thousands of specimens, the report became current that the American bison has 15 pairs of ribs, while his European cousin is blessed with only 14 pairs.

The true buffalo belongs to India and Africa, and differs from the bison in the absence of the hump on the shoulders and the long hair on the forepart of the body. (*See* Buffalo).

Bittern. The bittern was once a common bird in the eastern counties of England, but the draining of the fen country deprived him of most of his nesting haunts and so drove him to seek a home elsewhere. A few pairs remained for a number of years, but these were gradually reduced by hunters and egg collectors, till about the middle of last century the bittern could no longer be counted as a breeding species in Britain.

For about fifty years he was known only as a casual visitor to this country, but recently he has been encouraged to nest again by certain landowners who have strictly preserved the reed beds on their property and so have provided him for a number of seasons with a sanctuary in which he could live and breed in peace.

The bittern, *Botaurus stellaris*, belongs to the same tribe as the heron, *Ardeiformes*, but he has a much shorter neck and is more stoutly built than that bird. He spends his days among the reeds, and his plumage, which is buff marked with black, is so well suited to his surroundings that, though he is a large bird, over two feet in length and about three feet high, he is difficult to see so long as he remains still. His protection is made all the more complete by his strange habit of standing, when he is alarmed, with his long bill pointing straight up in the air.

Just like the heron he feeds on fish, frogs, water insects, etc. The nest is placed on the ground among the reeds, and, of course, is made of reeds. The eggs are laid in April or May, and so soon as one is laid the hen bird starts sitting, so that the young in the nest are of varying ages.

E. J. Hosking

BITTERN ACTS AS UMBRELLA

The bittern makes its nest among the reeds, and here one has been photographed as she stands over her nest to protect the young bird which has just hatched and the remaining eggs from a drenching shower of rain.

Unlike the heron, the bittern is a migratory bird. The American bittern, *B. lentiginosus*, sometimes visits this country, and so also does another species called the little bittern, *Ardella munila*.

The bittern's spring call is a loud booming note. He also has another call which is a kind of double croak.

Bittersweet. This extremely common plant of hedgerows and waste places throughout England and Ireland, may be recognized at once by its purple and yellow flowers, and also by the peculiarly shaped leaves. These have a large lobe like the blade of a spear, and two smaller ones more or less at right angles to it.

BEWARE BITTERSWEET!
This plant, also called " woody night-shade," is often confused with " deadly nightshade," and, like the latter, it is poisonous. On the right is an enlargement of the dangerous berries.
Photos, Bastin; Dennis

The bittersweet (*Solanum dulcamara*) is a member of the nightshade family (*Solanaceae*); it is also known as woody nightshade and sometimes, wrongly, as deadly nightshade. The blossoms give place to tempting-looking but poisonous egg-shaped berries about half an inch long, which turn from orange to red.

Björnson, BJÖRNSTJERNE. (Pron. byêrnst'-yêr-nā byêrn'-son). (1832–1910). The famous critic Georg Brandes once said of Björnson that " when his name is mentioned it is like hoisting the flag of Norway," for he was the most loved and the most representative of Norwegian writers. The author of Norway's national hymn, her greatest novelist, and, next to Ibsen, the greatest dramatist of his country, Björnson embodies the finest qualities of the Norwegian people.

He was born in Kvikne, a little village in central Norway, where his father was a Lutheran pastor. He was educated at the University of Christiania (Oslo), but left without taking his degree in order to devote himself to journalism. His first novel, " Synnöve Solbakken," published when he was 25, made a deep and lasting impression. It was the first of a series of tales of Norwegian peasant life, written in the simple and charming style of the old sagas. " Arne,"

published in the following year, is perhaps the best of all these stories ; it contains the beautiful song " Over the Lofty Mountains," which first showed Björnson's ability as a poet.

Björnson was also deeply interested in the drama. Two years after writing his first play he was made director of the theatre at Bergen, later becoming director of the National Theatre at Christiania (Oslo). In 1863 he was granted a government stipend to enable him to travel in Italy, France and Germany. He wrote a number of dramas based on the history of Norway, and then turned, like Ibsen, to the social problems of the day. He took a more hopeful view of these problems, however, than did Ibsen. As someone has said, while Ibsen expressed the doubt, Björnson expressed the faith of his people. He was less stern and cold, more gentle and sympathetic, than Ibsen.

As a newspaper writer and editor, and as a political orator, Björnson kept in close touch with the life about him and played a prominent part in the affairs of his day. A strong Nationalist, he helped to bring about the separation of Norway from Sweden, which took place in 1905. In 1903 he was awarded the Nobel prize for the most important literary work of that year. Long before his death his books had been translated into English and into many of the continental languages.

Among Björnson's best stories and novels are : " Synnöve Solbakken " (1857) ; " Arne " (1858); " The Heritage of the Kurts " (1884). His dramas include : " Between the Battles " (1855) ; " Sigurd Slembe " (1862) ; " Sigurd Jorsalfar " (1872) ; " The Gauntlet " (1883) ; " Beyond Our Powers " (Part I, 1883 ; Part II, 1895).

Blackberry. Not everyone knows that the blackberry plant or bramble is a cousin of the rose. But compare its flower with that of the common wild rose and you will see how alike they are. You will also see a strong family likeness between its leaves with their three or five large-toothed leaflets, and those of the rose with five or seven similar but smaller leaflets.

A still closer relative of the blackberry, *Rubus fruticosus*, is the raspberry, *Rubus idaeus*, which also grows wild in England. The blackberry has been cultivated of recent years, and more than 25 varieties have been developed, one thornless with white berries.

Blackbird. The sweet-songed blackbird—scientific name *Turdus merula*—belongs to the thrush family—*Turdidae*, of the order *Passeriformes*—though in colour it differs so much from the common thrush. The two birds are similar in size and form, and also in habits. But even in the plumage we can still find traces of their descent from the same forefathers. The adult cock blackbird has a beautiful black plumage and a bright orange bill, but the adult female is not black but brown, and her breast is lighter brown with dark markings. The young birds also are brown above, but this is profusely marked with buff spots, and their breasts are light brown with a dark tip to each feather. This spotted breast and the lighter markings on the upper parts, which are also possessed by the young thrush, may sometimes lead you to confuse the two species in the immature state.

The blackbird is one of our commonest birds, and for this we may well be grateful, for his song is the most beautiful of all our bird notes. He begins to sing at the end of February, and very soon afterwards is mated and making preparations for nesting. The nest is built of grass and mud, and lined with finer grass, and is usually placed in a hedge or low bush. The eggs are bluish-green, speckled with brown. There are usually four or five in a full clutch. As a rule a pair of blackbirds will raise two broods in the course of a season, but in mild springs they may have three and sometimes even four families.

Blackburn. An important part in the cotton trade has been played by this Lancashire town. It was one of the earliest towns in England where the factory system grew up, and it has always been in the front rank as regards improvements in manufacture. James Hargreaves, the inventor of the spinning-jenny, was a Blackburn man, and although his invention at first aroused much opposition, and even violence, on the part of the cotton operatives, it was afterwards acknowledged to mark a wonderful advance in the processes of manufacture, and proved of the greatest value to the industry. (*See* Arkwright, Richard; Hargreaves, James). The city has also important engineering works.

Unlike many modern factory towns, Blackburn was an important place long before it became one of the chief centres of the cotton trade. It is mentioned in Domesday Book, and it is believed that there was a Roman

C. W. Teager

THE MELODIOUS BLACKBIRD

There is no more welcome bird visitor to our gardens than the blackbird, for his song is one of the most musical sung by British birds. The cock, seen in this photograph, is all black save for his yellow bill. The hen is dark brown.

station, or camp, in the locality. Blackburn possesses a grammar school dating back to 1567, and boasting Queen Elizabeth as its foundress. The Gothic church of St. Mary, completed in 1826, is now the cathedral of the Bishop of Blackburn. Blackburn people are justly proud of their city, and the public buildings (which include a fine town hall) and public services are of the most modern kind. Population, 122,695.

Black Death. "I leave parchment for continuing the work if haply any man survive and if any of the race of Adam escape this pestilence." So wrote a despondent English monk in his chronicle while the terrible plague called the Black Death raged in England in 1349. And well might he despair, for this epidemic swept off at least one-quarter of the whole population of Europe.

The plague raged from 1348 to 1357. In France the ravages were as great as in England. "It is impossible to believe the number who have died throughout the whole country," wrote a French monk. "Travellers, merchants, pilgrims, declare that they have found cattle wandering without herdsmen in fields, towns and waste lands. They have seen barns and wine-cellars standing wide open, houses empty, and few people to be found anywhere. In many towns where there were before 20,000 people, scarcely 2,000 are left. In many places the fields lie uncultivated."

A person began to shiver, his temperature rose, swellings appeared in the neck, armpits or groin, and frequently death resulted in 12 hours.

In many ways the Black Death helped to bring the Middle Ages to a close. In England before the plague there were about four or five million inhabitants; when the pestilence had passed away there were only about half this number. Field labourers had become scarce, and those who were left demanded greatly increased wages. Many peasants left the estates of their masters and fled to the towns, or found places elsewhere where their lot was easier. Parliament passed laws to keep wages and prices at their former levels, but these could not be enforced. As a result the old manorial system of labour and agriculture broke down in England; in the new system the land was either rented to tenant farmers, or else it was retained by the lord and put into pasture for sheep and cattle.

The Black Death was only one of the many visitations of that disease which today we call the "bubonic plague." During the Pelopon-

nesian War it broke out in the city of Athens (430 B.C.). In the reign of the Roman Emperor Justinian grain-ships from Egypt brought it to Constantinople. Boccaccio places the scene of his "Decameron" on the hills about Florence, Italy, during the epidemic of 1348. Defoe describes the outbreak of 1665— the "Great Plague"—in London.

The home of bubonic plague is in Asia, and we now know that it is carried by a certain kind of flea which lives on rats. With the advance of medical science and sanitation its ravages have been checked in the western world, but constant vigilance is still required on the part of health officers at seaports to prevent its revival.

Black Forest, GERMANY.
Scores of German nursery tales tell of the dwarfs and elves and fairies that were supposed to haunt every valley and wooded height in the famous Black Forest of Germany.

The Black Forest lies in the elbow formed by the river Rhine as it flows westward from Lake Constance and turns sharply to the north. Stretching away to the north—mile after mile—are the rounded mountains, crowned with stately pines and firs. The trees support a dome of dark green foliage, giving in the half-light an appearance not unlike the interior of a great cathedral, although no human

craftsman ever fashioned so magnificent a temple. There are two lakes, both ancient volcanic craters, and as they are very deep and still they give a perfect reflection of the trees around.

In the narrow valleys lie snug hamlets scattered along the streams, while here and there are isolated dwellings, partly hidden by fruit trees, looking down from sunny slopes or projecting their quaint gables from a forest background. The length of the chain is about 100 miles and its average width is 24 miles. The loftiest elevation is the round-topped Feldberg, 4,898 feet high. To one coming from the towering snow-capped peaks of the Alps, the Black Forest seems but a mass of gentle wooded hills.

The woodlands of this region are beautifully kept. A tree felled by the wind or blasted by

MÄDCHEN OF THE BLACK FOREST
In the valleys between the forested slopes of that part of southern Germany called the "Schwarzwald" (Black Forest) are many little villages and towns that seem to have changed little in life, or architecture, or dress, for three hundred years. In such villages live these girls (the German word for "girls" is "mädchen")
Photos, German Travel Bureau; Haeckel

lightning is immediately removed, and all broken twigs and branches are used for fuel.

Here and there are nurseries in which each spring are planted the seeds of a future forest. The pine and fir predominate, but in order to provide for every locality, other varieties are sown, such as maple, ash, birch, walnut, and even fruit trees. The groves planted by one generation are cared for by the next, and are cut down and sawed into lumber by the third.

The beautiful Danube and Neckar rivers rise in these mountains. Along these and other streams are little manufacturing towns, where wooden articles, cuckoo-clocks, musical-boxes, and toys are made. Cattle graze on the grassy slopes, and the beauty of the region makes the Black Forest a favourite summer tourist resort. The greater part of the Black Forest is included in the state of Baden. (*See* Baden).

Black Sea.

This great sea, one-sixth as large as the Mediterranean—with which it is connected by the Bosporus, the Sea of Marmara (Marmora) and the Dardanelles—lies between Asia Minor on the south and Russia on the north, and between Bulgaria and Rumania on the west and the region of the Caucasus Mountains on the east, and so plays its part in separating —and in uniting—Europe and Asia.

For over 2,000 years its waters have been traversed by ships of early traders, pirates and settlers, and by vessels of modern commerce and war. For Russia the navigation of this sea, with its Mediterranean outlets, is a vital necessity, and it has figured since the 18th century in that country's history. The fact that the Turks were able to block the entrance at the Dardanelles in the World War of 1914-18 tended to prolong that contest and contributed to the discomfort of Russia.

Including the Sea of Azov (Azof), which is really a gulf of the Black Sea, almost enclosed by the Crimea and entered through the Strait of Kertch or Yenikale, the surface area is about 170,000 square miles, that of the Sea of Azov being 14,500 sq. miles. Its greatest length is 750 miles, its greatest width is 380 miles, and its greatest depth, 7,350 feet. It has no islands of importance and practically no tides.

The Black Sea drains nearly one-quarter of the surface of Europe. This large inflow of fresh water makes it much less salt than the ocean or even the Mediterranean, and sets up a peculiar current. In the upper level of the Black Sea the fresh water flows outward towards the Bosporus, while in the lower levels the current from the Aegean Sea flows in the opposite direction. Some of the great rivers which find their outlet in the Black Sea are the Danube, the Dniester, the Bug, the Dnieper, the Don (through the Sea of Azov), and the Kuban. The larger ports include Odessa, Kherson, Sebastopol, Trebizond and Sinope.

The Black Sea has the reputation of being dangerous to navigation, especially during the season of winter storms. But it is now believed that the Black Sea is no worse in this respect than other inland seas. It is usually free of ice, even in the coldest weather.

The Black Sea has been navigated from very early periods. The Greeks colonized its shores as early as the 7th century B.C. After the Turks captured Constantinople, in 1453, they closed

THE BLACK SEA BETWEEN EUROPE AND ASIA MINOR

Draining nearly a fourth of Europe, the Black Sea just had to be big ! In summer its disposition is sunny, but in winter it gets as cross as a big black bear. Imprisoned within those mountain walls, the winds are set whirling in a vast turmoil, which causes trouble for vessels. It's a tempest in a tea-pot, in a way ; but what a tea-pot—380 miles wide, 750 miles long, and 7,350 feet deep in some places! Probably no body of water of similar size, in spite of ancient belief, is safer for navigators.

the sea to all but their own ships, though later Russia obtained certain rights. Today, by a convention signed in 1936, merchant and naval vessels even of non-Black Sea Powers may pass through the refortified Dardanelles into the sea.

Blake, ROBERT (1599–1657). The memory of the great Admiral Blake is dear to the British people, not only for his naval glory and success, but even more for the tradition of his chivalrous character and his unselfish patriotism.

Like Sir Francis Drake, Blake grew up in the West Country—at Bridgwater, in Somerset —but spent some years studying at Oxford University. He left Oxford in 1625, and little is known of him for the next fifteen years— probably he was trading and gaining experience at sea. In 1640 he was chosen by his Puritan fellow-townsmen as their representative in the Short Parliament.

Blake's great qualities of leadership first shone with brilliancy when the Civil War broke out in 1642. He at once joined the Parliamentary forces and drew favourable attention to himself, chiefly through the seizure and year-long defence of Taunton, which enabled the Parliamentary party to maintain itself in the west of England for a considerable time.

Blake was now asked to assume a high command in the Navy and pursue the royalists who had taken to the sea. He at once built up a fleet and proceeded to hunt the royalists from the high seas. At Cartagena he caught and destroyed the greater portion of their vessels and succeeded in capturing their last stronghold, the Scilly Islands.

Blake was then called upon to lead the English fleets in their mighty struggle for the mastery of the seas against the Dutch under De Ruyter and Van Tromp, who was cruising, according to the story, with a broom at his masthead to indicate that he had swept the seas clear of Englishmen.

Blake Ever in the Van

In battle Blake showed the same daring and heroic endurance that had already marked him out. He was repeatedly in the most extreme danger, was once severely wounded, and much of the time he suffered painfully from disease. In spite of all, however, Blake and the other English leaders triumphed, and Van Tromp was defeated. The English, for the time being, had established their naval supremacy.

The last exploit of the great admiral was his greatest and most daring—the crushing defeat

AN INCIDENT IN THE LIFE OF BRAVE ADMIRAL BLAKE

" I would have you and all the world know that none but an Englishman shall chastise an Englishman." These are the word that Blake is addressing to the Spaniard, who has demanded the right to punish a British seaman who had been guilty of un gentlemanly conduct on shore. The incident occurred during the operations in the Mediterranean Sea in 1655. The origina painting is by A. D. McCormick, R.I.

Permission of City of Plymouth Museum and Art Gallery

in 1656 of a Spanish fleet off the Canary Islands under the guns of a castle and six or seven forts. This exploit excited great enthusiasm in England and admiration throughout Europe. After this his health failed rapidly, and he died on his way home as he was sailing into the harbour of Plymouth. Blake received a magnificent public funeral and was buried in Westminster Abbey, but in 1660 his body was exhumed and re-interred in the churchyard of St. Margaret's, Westminster.

Blake, WILLIAM (1757–1827). In a single room in a humble part of London, William Blake, by a process of his own, etched words on copper, decorated the plates with designs of singular beauty, and added an occasional full-page picture. The book was "Songs of Innocence," a collection of poems written by Blake himself. The illustrations were from his paintings. He blended the ink, ground the colours, and mixed his own paint. Catherine, his wife, made impressions, tinted the prints, and bound them neatly in boards. They must have

FROM ONE OF BLAKE'S BOOKS
Here is the title page, drawn by William Blake, from one of his two famous books, " Songs of Innocence " and "Songs of Experience." First editions of these books are very valuable; though they are little larger than a pocket-book the two volumes have been sold recently for as much as £1,700.

laughed gaily together when the first volume was finished, for they had made everything but the paper ! That was in 1789, and the book sold for a few shillings. Today a copy is worth hundreds of pounds.

William Blake, poet, artist, designer and mystic, was born in London, Nov. 28, 1757, the son of a hosier. He developed his talent for sketching at a drawing school and by collecting prints of old masters. At 14 he was apprenticed to an engraver ; at 24 he had married and opened a print-seller's shop. In the poetry and painting of his leisure hours he developed a haunting mysticism whose beauty was not appreciated until long after he was dead. All his life he had visions. When he was four years old he remarked that he " saw God put His forehead to the window," and three years later he barely escaped a flogging from his father for saying that he had seen a tree full of angels. When he grew older these visions gave to his painting extraordinary power, for he saw everything before he put his designs on paper. Publishers took advantage of him ; rival artists stole his ideas and reaped rich profits while Blake himself fared poorly. He died Aug. 12, 1827, and was buried in an unmarked grave. Not until 100 years later, in 1927, was a tablet erected over his supposed resting place.

" Songs of Innocence " and its later companion volume, "Songs of Experience," are his best-known works. The second includes his famous " Tiger ! Tiger ! Burning Bright." In 1804 Blake published " Jerusalem," later set to music as a hymn by Parry.

Blake's fame as an artist and master of design rests largely on a set of copperplate etchings, his dramatic interpretation of the Book of Job. He illustrated Richard Gough's massive work, " Sepulchral Monuments of Great Britain," produced between 1786 and 1796. For his models he spent hours in the dim vaulted aisles of Westminster Abbey, copying the figures.

Blast-furnace. Used to extract the iron from the ore, a blast-furnace looks like the funnel of a great steamship, but tapers upwards. Coke, iron-ore and limestone are carried to the mouth of the furnace by elevators raised by hydraulic pressure or electrical appliances, which have taken the place of the pneumatic hoists formerly used. The furnace is fed with alternate layers of coke and iron-ore. The furnace is about 25 ft. across. At the bottom end it is possible to see the fire through observation holes covered with coloured glass.

The terrific heat inside the furnace is obtained by blowing the fire with a very strong and continuous blast of heated air. The gases provided by the furnace are used not only to heat the air in the blast, but also for raising steam to force

BLAST-FURNACE EXTRACTING IRON FROM ORE

A MOUTHFUL FOR THE FURNACE

FURNACE MOUTH

PIPE CARRYING GAS TO STOVE AND ENGINES

COKE
LIMESTONE
ORE
COKE
LIMESTONE
ORE
COKE
LIMESTONE
ORE
COKE
LIMESTONE
ORE
COKE
LIMESTONE
ORE
COKE
LIMESTONE
ORE
COKE

SLAG
MOLTEN IRON

PIPE FOR DRAWING OFF SLAG

PIPE FOR DRAWING OFF IRON

IRON ORE

COKE

LIMESTONE

BUCKETS WAITING TO BE EMPTIED INTO FURNACE

In this diagram a blast-furnace is shown as though it had been cut in two from top to bottom. Coke, limestone and ore are brought up the inclined track and dropped in alternate layers into the furnace. When melted the limestone and the impurities in the iron are united to make what is called slag, and both the slag and the iron-ore sink to the bottom of the furnace. The slag, being lighter, floats on the top of the molten ore and both are drawn off at intervals through the drain-pipes. So that no heat may be lost hot air is pumped into the bottom of the furnace, the engines that pump in the air being run on the gas from the top of the furnace. Inset is the exterior of a furnace like that shown in the diagram.

the hot air into the furnace through pipes six feet in diameter, and at a pressure which would blow a person away like a piece of paper.

Every three hours the molten iron is tapped from the base of the furnace, and as it runs forth like a fiery serpent, it is guided into channels fashioned in sand, where it is allowed to cool and form blocks, or pigs, of iron—hence the name pig-iron. The work continues day and night, and the furnace never goes out except when it is necessary to make repairs.

Bleaching. The process that gives cotton, linen and other fabrics the snow-white appearance they usually have is called bleaching. Formerly cotton and linen fabrics were bleached by repeated boilings in caustics and lyes and exposure to the sun. This process, in which the Dutch excelled in the 18th century, was shortened from several months to a few days by the the discovery, in 1790, of the bleaching powers of chlorine gas in contact with water.

The most important bleaching agent is the chlorine compound known as chloride of lime, or "bleaching powder." When dissolved in water it releases oxygen. This unites with the colouring matter and forms a white compound, which either dissolves in water and is washed out, or remains in the fabric. Other chemicals that act in a similar way are peroxide of hydrogen, peroxide of sodium, and potash permanganate, used for straw and jute.

Fabrics of vegetable origin are usually bleached with such oxidizing agents ; wool and silk with reducing agents, that is, those which absorb oxygen. However, peroxide of hydrogen, a powerful oxidizer, is valuable for bleaching silk as well as vegetable fibres.

Blenheim, BATTLE OF. Blenheim village, in Bavaria, on the Danube, is not so well known, perhaps, as the mansion of Blenheim, and its princely estate, in Oxfordshire. The estate, together with half a million pounds, was granted by England to the Duke of Marlborough for his services in defeating the French

and the Bavarians at the battle of Blenheim on August 13, 1704. Robert Southey wrote a poem on the battle, and he very truthfully and wittily hits off its importance in the last verse :

'And everybody praised the Duke
Who this great fight did win.' ˙
'But what good came of it at last ? '
Quoth little Peterkin.
'Why, that I cannot tell,' said he,
'But 'twas a famous victory ! '

Marlborough began the battle by ordering his infantry to attack the French, who had taken up their position behind a strong defence of palisades. The British suffered severe losses in the earlier encounters, and at 5 p.m. it seemed as if the French would be the victors. Marlborough, however, asked the Austrian leader, Prince Eugene, to send assistance, and the united forces checked the French and made it possible for the cavalry to advance. This move put the whole army into confusion.

MARLBOROUGH'S MEN AT BLENHEIM

The artist here shows the great Duke of Marlborough's army advancing against the French at the Battle of Blenheim in 1704. In those days soldiers fought abroad in the same uniforms that they wore on parade at home. They advanced in close formation, led by officers with drawn swords. The colours were carried into action, and efforts to capture them were often the cause of fierce hand-to-hand fighting. The drums and bugles were also in the front line.

Blériot, LOUIS. (Pron. blär′iō). (1872–1936). On July 25, 1909, England ceased to be a real island, for on that day Blériot crossed the English Channel in his aeroplane.

At dawn Blériot was ready on the beach at Baraques, near Calais, beside his tiny, frail monoplane, the precious product of ten years' experiments. "Dîtes-moi, où est Douvres ? " ("Tell me, where is Dover ? "), he asked, and on being shown its rough direction, he took off and headed out to sea with nothing to guide him but an escorting destroyer.

"*Daily Mirror*"

ACROSS THE CHANNEL: BLÉRIOT'S HOUR OF TRIUMPH

Louis Blériot accomplished the first aeroplane flight over the English Channel on July 25, 1909; and when the news was heard of his landing on the cliffs near Dover, a few far-seeing people realized that England had to all intents and purposes ceased to be an island. Here is the airman (in flying suit) standing beside his monoplane, through the fuselage of which the French tricolour has been "planted." A memorial tablet now marks this historic spot.

Soon, however, Blériot left even the destroyer behind and his safety now depended on his aeroplane and its 25 h.p. engine. He remembered the almost tragic result of Latham's attempt six days before—engine-failure and a descent into the Channel. But all went well with Blériot, and 40 minutes after the start he landed on the cliffs near Dover at a place now marked by a stone tablet.

In after years Blériot became famous as an aircraft constructor, and many of his machines were used by the French in the World War. He died on August 1, 1936.

Blight. When plants dry up and shrivel, or turn yellowish or brown, or when the fruit decays early, there has probably been an attack of "blight." Often this is caused by a mildew attacking the leaves, but it may be primarily due to a poor supply of food and air at the roots.

Blights of grains are called "rusts" or "smuts," because they make the grain look reddish or black. Other common blights are "scab" and "rot" of potatoes, "beetroot rot," "peach-leaf curl," and "apple scab."

Blind, EDUCATION OF THE. No more pitiful plight for a two-year-old child can be imagined than to be blind, deaf and dumb. This was the situation of a little American girl, Laura Bridgman (born in 1829), about a hundred years ago; but, nevertheless, she became a cheerful, happy citizen and did a great deal for the happiness of others.

When she was eight years old Dr. Samuel G. Howe, superintendent of the Perkins Institute for the Blind in Boston, U.S.A.,

undertook successfully the untried task of developing a mind thus doubly barred. First, the child was given a spoon and a fork on which were labels with the raised letters F-O-R-K and S-P-O-O-N. Gradually the connexion dawned upon her, and when the labels were removed she could replace them on the proper articles. Then the letters were separated, and patiently she was taught to assemble them so that they would spell the words. This process was repeated with other articles, until finally she was familiar with the whole alphabet, and knew how to spell many names of simple objects.

Now she was ready to learn finger-spelling. A raised letter would be given to her, and, with Laura's delicate fingers "watching" closely, the deaf-and-dumb sign of that letter would be formed by the teacher. Soon she was "writing her thoughts on the air" with astonishing rapidity, and by feeling with her hands the signs made by the person conversing with her, she was soon "talking" with them. This education continued until she was 20 years old, and she developed into a skilful teacher of blind children and was happily employed earning her own living until her death in 1889.

Laura Bridgman did not have the brilliant mind of that other famous blind deaf-mute, Helen Keller, who was also trained by Dr. Howe, and did not achieve such spectacular results. (*See* Keller, Helen.) But her education was the greatest accomplishment of the comparatively new art of teaching those similarly afflicted. Up to the beginning of the 19th century scarcely any attempt had been made to ease the lot of the blind and to teach them to support themselves. Today by far the greater number of blind persons in progressive countries are educated, independent, self-supporting citizens. For this change much of the credit is due to the blind themselves—to their eagerness to learn and their untiring devotion to their tasks.

Books for the blind are now for the most part not printed in raised letters, but in an alphabet of raised " points." This method was invented in 1829 by Louis Braille, who became one of the best organists in Paris, and a noted educator of the blind. As a child he delighted to play in his father's saddlery shop, punching holes in the scraps of leather with an awl. One day, when he was three years of age, the sharp tool slipped, injuring his eye so severely that he became totally blind.

He thought a great deal about the little marks the awl left in the leather, and the idea came that if the awl were punched only half-way through, a dot would be raised on the other side. With this as a basis Braille worked out a system whereby different variations of groups of little raised dots represented letters of the alphabet, special word and syllable signs, and punctuation marks. Educators seized upon this system, and with modifications it is taught in every country where there are schools for the blind. To persons whose fingers are not sensitive, it

seems as it did to the newly blinded soldier, who, running his fingers over the page, exclaimed disgustedly, " It feels just like a sheet of sandpaper." But to thousands who have mastered its characters it has opened a new world of happiness. Books printed in Braille, besides being much bulkier than ordinary books, are much more expensive, so that the vast majority of the blind depend for their literature on libraries supported by public subscription.

LEAVES OF A BRAILLE BOOK
One disadvantage of Braille books is that they are necessarily cumbersome. In order to lessen the bulk, however, characters are embossed on both sides of the page, the lines of dots on one side falling between those on the other side.

Typewriters have been invented for writing Braille, and machines for embossing the characters on brass plates, so that any number of impressions may be printed.

For writing Braille by hand, a grooved board is used with a perforated metal rule to serve as a guide, and the points are impressed on soft paper with a metal pencil. This is read on the reverse side. Writing Braille is a tedious process, so in most institutions for the blind the use of the Braille typewriter is also taught. The " touch " system, now universally used by typists, was originally devised for the blind. Special touch devices are employed to teach geography, arithmetic and natural history to the blind.

One of the most wonderful recent inventions is the phonopticon. This is a device for converting light impulses into sound, so that the blind may *hear* the books they cannot see. (*See* Light).

HOW THE BLIND READ
This photograph of a Braille library gives an idea how large Braille books are ; but despite their size several volumes are needed for a book of even moderate length. The librarian is here seen literally " dipping into a book."

Not a few blind persons are engaged in farming. Many of them excel as musicians, and a considerable proportion become piano-tuners. Basketry and broom-making are other occupations especially suited to the blind, while many of the blind take to healing their fellow men and women by becoming masseurs. In Great Britain the four principal institutions which look after the welfare of the blind are the National Institute for the Blind, which co-ordinates all the efforts to assist those who have lost their sight; the Royal Normal College, which gives a good general education to blind pupils of both sexes; the National Library for the Blind, which makes and circulates Braille books; and St. Dunstan's Hostel, Regent's Park, which was founded by the late Sir C. Arthur Pearson to look after the welfare of soldiers blinded in the World War. The present chairman of St. Dunstan's, Sir Ian Fraser, who was himself blinded in the World War, was subsequently called to the Bar, and became a member of Parliament and a Governor of the British Broadcasting Corporation.

Blockade.

When the coast of a country at war is patrolled by enemy ships to break its sea communications it is said to be blockaded. During the Civil War in America, the most daring sea captains of the Confederacy were employed in trying to break through the lines of northern warships which blockaded the southern seaports. At night their low black-painted ships, usually loaded with cotton for the British market, would steal out of the harbours and dash for the open sea. The war measure which closed the southern ports and ultimately starved out the Confederacy is an historic example of the naval operation known as blockade. It extended even to neutral ships, which were liable to seizure if they tried to break into a blockaded port.

In the Declaration of Paris, agreed to by the Great Powers in 1856, the principle was laid down that fighting nations could not declare an enemy port blockaded unless they actually carried out the blockade with warships patrolling the approaches to the harbour. "A blockade, in order to be binding, must be effective, that is to say, maintained by a force sufficient really to prevent access to the coast of an enemy," was the way the agreement read.

During the World War of 1914–18 sea-mines, submarines, and the development of long-range guns for coast defence made it impossible for the Allies to carry out an actual blockade of the ports of the Central Powers. So the principle of 1856 was modified, and an "embargo" or "long-range blockade" of the enemy countries was declared.

In February, 1915, the Germans declared a submarine blockade of the British Isles. This meant that their submarines would sink without warning all ships entering the North Sea and other surrounding seas. Great losses were caused to British and neutral shipping, for submarines, unlike surface ships, cannot take seamen prisoner and put them in safety; but after a tremendous effort the danger was largely overcome. This ruthless action on the part of Germany did a great deal towards inducing the United States to join the Allies. (*See* World War of 1914–18).

BLONDIN ABOVE NIAGARA'S ABYSS

Blondin's most famous feat was to walk on a tight-rope over Niagara Falls carrying a man on his back. It required perhaps greater courage on the part of the passenger than on that of the tight-rope walker !

Blondin, CHARLES

(1824–1897). The name of Charles Blondin—his real name was Jean François Gravelet—will go down in history owing to that marvellous feat which he successfully accomplished in 1859, when he walked on a tight-rope across the falls of Niagara. Blondin was a Frenchman, a born showman, and such was the world-wide fame which he gained by walking across Niagara on a rope that he repeated the feat a good many times, with variations—blindfold, pushing a wheelbarrow, carrying a man on his back, and so forth.

Blondin made a great deal of money by this and similar acrobatic performances, and afterwards spent most of his life in England. He gave many performances at the Crystal Palace and elsewhere, and was naturally very popular with the public, especially with the boys and girls, who were greatly thrilled by his daring and wonderful nerve. Notwithstanding the dangerous nature of his work, Blondin was seventy-three years of age when he died at Ealing.

The BLOOD STREAM in our BODIES

The drop of blood that appears when you prick your finger marks a leak in that most marvellous mechanism, the circulatory system in your body. How the blood stream works, and the corpuscles comprising it, are described below.

Blood. A spot of blood examined under a microscope shows that it is made up of a liquid, called the " plasma," in which float millions of tiny round bodies. These are living cells and are of two kinds. One kind is red and is called the " red corpuscle " (*erythrocyte*). A single drop of blood no larger than a pin's head contains several millions of these minute bodies. They are manufactured in the marrow of the bones and the spleen, and are the oxygen carriers. The other kind of cell is white and is known as the " white corpuscle " (*leucocyte*).

The white corpuscles are outnumbered by the red by almost four hundred to one. They are somewhat larger in size and possess the power of changing form and of creeping. They gather particles of foreign substance, and creep with them out of the blood-vessels, and even to the surface of the body. They feed upon bacteria, and help to rid the body of disease germs. They are therefore the scavengers of the blood. They are renewed from the spleen and lymphatic glands. A microscopic examination of the blood to note the condition of white or red corpuscles is often necessary as an indication of disease or health in the body as a whole, as, for instance, in malaria.

The plasma is a very complex liquid. It contains food products on their way to be used in various organs, and also waste materials on their way to the organs of removal. It is moreover the bearer of hormones, those wonderful stimulating products of the ductless glands. In general, the purpose of the blood is to supply every part of the body with what it needs, and remove what it does not need.

The plasma has a peculiar characteristic which is extremely useful. If a blood-vessel is cut or broken so that the blood is escaping, there is a substance in the plasma called *fibrin* which entangles the corpuscles in its meshes and forms a clot ; otherwise we might bleed to death. This process is called coagulation. If a person loses a large quantity of blood, his life can be saved by blood transfusion, which is the injection of blood from some other person into his vessels.

Transfusions Must Mix

Since there are four different types of human blood a sample of the donor's blood and of the patient's must be tested beforehand to see whether the types are compatible. Transfusion of bloods that do not mix freely may cause agglutination, or the lumping together of the red cells, with fatal results.

The weight of the blood is approximately one-twentieth that of the body.

The heart is a double action pumping-plant. (*See* Heart). The left side pumps oxygenated or " arterial " blood all over the body. This blood loses much of its oxygen in passing through the living organs, and at the same time collects a waste product called carbon dioxide. This

HARVEY DEMONSTRATES THE CIRCULATION OF THE BLOOD

William Harvey, an English physician, discovered the circulation of the blood in 1616 ; and here he is seen explaining his discovery to King Charles I. Previously it was thought that the blood moved irregularly throughout the body, but Harvey showed that the heart is a pump systematically and regularly circulating the blood through the arteries. Harvey, like many pioneers in medical science, received much criticism and even contradiction before his theory was finally accepted.

"used up" blood comes back to the right side of the heart as "venous" blood. The right side pumps this venous blood through the lungs. There it takes up oxygen again and loses carbon dioxide, and then passes back to the left side of the heart as arterial blood. Thus the blood is constantly going out and always coming back to the same place, moving—as Harvey, the discoverer of the circulation, said—"in a circle, as it were." This discovery of the circulation of the blood by the English physician, Harvey, marked an epoch in medical science.

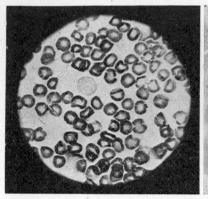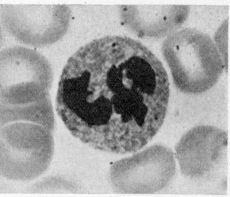

RED AND WHITE CORPUSCLES OF THE BLOOD

On the left are seen red corpuscles (erythrocytes) and on the right a white corpuscle (leucocyte) in the centre, surrounded by reds. Note that the white corpuscle has a nucleus, while the non-nuclear reds are concave on both sides. These photographs are highly magnified, that on the right being 5,000 times actual size.

Right photo, courtesy F. Davidson & Co.

The passage from the left side of the heart throughout the body and back to the right side is called the " systemic " circulation ; while the passage through the lungs is known as the " pulmonary " circulation. All this necessitates three sets of pipes or blood-vessels. Those which carry blood *from* the heart are called " arteries," and those which carry blood *to* the heart are called " veins." The extremely small—indeed, microscopic—tubes connecting the arteries and veins are called " capillaries."

There are millions of capillaries, which in one sense are the most important vessels, for in them the exchanges of food and waste take place.

We have spoken of oxygen and carbon dioxide as examples of usable and waste materials. It is on the basis of the relative proportions of these two gases that arterial blood is often called " pure " and venous blood " impure." But it should be borne in mind that many other kinds of usable material, mostly so-called foods, and many kinds of waste are collected and distributed. Thus it happens that venous blood from the intestinal wall during digestion may contain more food than the arterial blood

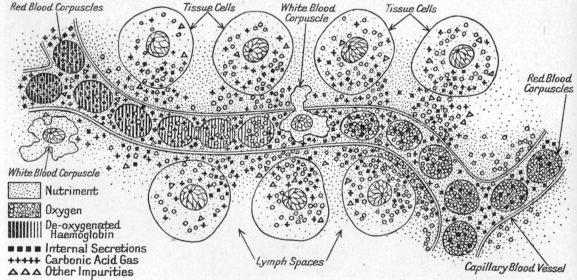

Red Blood Corpuscles   Tissue Cells   White Blood Corpuscle   Tissue Cells   Red Blood Corpuscles

White Blood Corpuscle

▒ Nutriment
▓ Oxygen
▥ De-oxygenated Haemoglobin
■■■■ Internal Secretions
+++++ Carbonic Acid Gas
△△△ Other Impurities

Lymph Spaces   Capillary Blood Vessel

HOW THE BLOOD NOURISHES AND CLEANSES THE BODY TISSUES

This diagram explains the important rôles played by the circulation in the microscopic blood vessels known as capillaries. Consult the key to the symbols used. On the right are red corpuscles full of oxygen, nutriment and internal secretions which they give out to the tissue cells lying outside the capillary. In return they receive carbon dioxide (carbonic acid gas), de-oxygenated haemoglobin (colouring of red corpuscles) and other impurities which they carry to the veins on the left. Note the white blood corpuscle on the left which has passed through the capillary wall, and another, in centre, passing through.

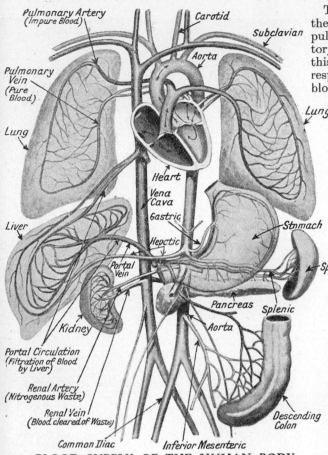

Pulmonary Artery (Impure Blood)
Carotid
Subclavian
Aorta
Pulmonary Vein (Pure Blood)
Lung
Heart
Vena Cava
Gastric
Liver
Hepatic
Stomach
Portal Vein
Spleen
Pancreas
Splenic
Aorta
Kidney
Portal Circulation (Filtration of Blood by Liver)
Descending Colon
Renal Artery (Nitrogenous Waste)
Renal Vein (Blood cleared of Waste)
Common Iliac
Inferior Mesenteric

BLOOD SUPPLY OF THE HUMAN BODY

The right side of the heart receives impure venous blood from all parts of the body and pumps it through the lungs ; the left side receives purified blood from the lungs and sends it back through the body. This completes the process of circulation.

supplied to the same organs. The venous blood from the kidney is purer as regards certain waste substances than the arterial blood, and so on. The blood in every part differs slightly from every other part. The circulation leads to a constant renewal, purification and mixing of the blood, so that every part gets what it needs and gets rid of what it does not need.

Ordinarily the flow of blood to the different organs is very exactly regulated without any conscious work on our part. That is, the organ which is working hardest will receive a greater proportion of blood at the time than the one that is at rest. But we may consciously increase or change the rate of flow from one organ to another by increasing the activity of that organ. This is true chiefly in regard to the voluntary muscles. We may seriously interfere with the circulation by taking anything into the system which will interfere with the heart action or with blood-vessels, such as drugs of various kinds.

The force of gravity is always acting on the blood, as upon any liquid, tending to pull it into the lowest parts of the circulatory system. Under usual circumstances this is compensated for, and head and feet respectively get their proper amounts of blood. Sometimes the nervous regulation is defective, the blood is drawn away from the brain and the person faints. A fainting patient will recover if he is laid flat on the ground, preferably with the feet raised, so that gravity pulls the blood back into the brain. Through circulation also the temperature of the body is adjusted. If we are warm, more blood goes to the skin. If we are cold, the blood is kept inside and heat loss diminished. (*See also* the articles on Heart; Physiology; and Respiration).

Ancient physicians believed that the arteries contained air, and only the veins blood. The Greek physician Galen, in the second century A.D. demonstrated that both arteries and veins contain blood; but he thought the blood went out and back in the arteries—a kind of ebb and flow—and similarly for the veins, with a different kind of blood. A direct connexion between arteries and veins was not thought of. In 1628 Dr. William Harvey, of London, published a book in which he proved that the quantity of blood leaving the heart and the rate at which it leaves made a return to the heart necessary. He did not, however, actually see the minute capillaries which connect arteries and veins. It remained for the Italian Malpighi, in 1661, and the Hollander Leeuwenhoek, in 1669, to demonstrate with the microscope the existence of these minute tubes connecting arteries and veins.

Blood, THOMAS (died 1680). Having been deprived of his estates at the Restoration in 1660, this Irish soldier of fortune, who was known as " Colonel " Blood, tried to seize Dublin Castle and to carry off Ormonde, the Lord-Lieutenant. The plot failed and some of his associates were executed, but Blood himself managed to escape. He made another attempt on Ormonde's life, but this also was unsuccessful. His next and most famous exploit was stealing the crown jewels from the Tower of London. Disguised as a clergyman, he entered the Tower and carried off the crown under his cloak, while two of his associates made off with the orb and the sceptre. Meanwhile, the keeper of the jewels, who had been seriously maltreated by the ruffians, recovered sufficiently to give the alarm, and the whole gang were captured with the jewels in their

BLUEBELL CARPET IN A WOODLAND GLADE

Fox

Blu bells are found all over Western Europe, and they rival the primroses as the most familiar of British wild flowers in sprin They chiefly flourish in woodlands, and such a scene as this, when the light filters through the trees on to a mass of the bl blossoms, is one of the most delightful that the countryside can offer. Bluebells are far more beautiful in such a setting tha when they are used to decorate a room, and the lover of flowers is content to see them thus and refrains from plucking then